JOSEF BOR, like his father before him, was an outstanding lawyer and a leader among the Jews in prewar Czechoslovakia. In 1942, in a mass reprisal for the assassination of "Reichsprotektor" Heydrich, he and his family were sent, together with other Jews, to a newly established Nazi concentration camp in the fortress town of Terezín (Theresienstadt). Of his entire family, he alone survived, not only Terezín but Auschwitz-Birkenau and Buchenwald as well. His first work, *THE ABANDONED DOLL,* an autobiographical novel, was written when he was over fifty years old, and has been a great success in Czechoslovakia. Later, at the urging of surviving fellow prisoners, he wrote *THE TEREZIN REQUIEM,* in which he pays homage to the memory of Raphael Schachter and the nameless five hundred artists who helped him perform Verdi's *Requiem.*

THE
TEREZÍN
REQUIEM

JOSEF BOR

Translated from
The Czech by
EDITH PARGETER

 A BARD BOOK/PUBLISHED BY AVON BOOKS

Original Czech version entitled *Terezínské Requiem,* © Josef
Bor 1963; Ceskoslovensky Spisovatel, Prague.

AVON BOOKS
A division of
The Hearst Corporation
959 Eighth Avenue
New York, New York 10019

First Bard Printing, March, 1978

BARD TRADEMARK REG. U.S. PAT. OFF. AND IN
OTHER COUNTRIES, MARCA REGISTRADA, HECHO EN
U.S.A.

Printed in the U.S.A.

THE
TEREZÍN
REQUIEM

THE summer of the year 1944 was a time of storm. The shattered and demoralized German armies were retreating on all fronts, the German cities were transformed into heaps of bizarre ruins, and Hitler, inflamed into open madness by the attempt on his life, scattered death in the ranks of the *Wehrmacht*. The Nazi empire was collapsing to its very foundations.

None of this interfered with Eichmann's plans. The tactics of his "final solution of the Jewish problem" in the field of Central Europe remained unchanged. Construction was completed on the strictly secret and perfectly disguised Birkenau work camp at Neu Berun, which had a capacity of ten thousand human bodies per twenty-four hours. And the chief device by which the disguise was maintained, a great assembly camp, the ghetto of Terezín, heretofore a place of suffering, hunger, and death, was in the short space of a few weeks rebuilt and decked out into a gigantic, astonishing film set, commissioned for the penultimate act of the tragedy of Terezín. In accordance with Eichmann's scenario, living people had to help create this film set. And they believed in it; they began to hope and to live.

In the yard of the former Terezín school, before the closed doors of the large auditorium, a great crowd of people was patiently standing. They were waiting for the artists to enter the hall first, for later they would have found difficulty in getting in at all. And here they came, Raphael Schächter and his entire company, and the crowd welcomed him warmly and without ceremony, in the manner of good friends who greet each other every day in the street. The gulf between audience and artist did not exist between them; they were all prisoners of one camp.

"Hey, Raphael, you'd better show us something today," they cried out to the conductor. No one here ever addressed him in any other way; the whole ghetto knew him by that name. "Come on, get on with it!" they shouted encouragingly from all sides, and the artists smiled and nodded. "It's going to be first class, boys, we won't let you down."

Schächter unlocked the doors, and the artists entered and went straight to their places. There was no platform here; only a turned-up bench stood at the conductor's music stand to act as a rostrum for him. Schächter mounted it, and stood watching as the hall filled.

In they came, children and grownups together, for even the children understood the music to be performed today; in the ghetto, death was always all around them. Many old people came, too, thin and bent, in tattered and much mended clothes. Even beggars . . . And these were the very ones who had tried most valiantly, in making their appearance in public, to express in some way the ceremonial character of today's *première*, if only by a length of narrow ribbon worn in place of a tie.

There were no ushers in the hall; everyone knew very well where he had to go. There was space reserved for the children on the floor around the orchestra, the older people crowded closely on the long benches, and the younger adults thronged along the walls and the aisles.

Was there still space for one more soul to enter? It was quite full here already; it seemed impossible for anyone else to get in. But still Schächter waited patiently, and into the hall pressed more people, and still more. Incredible how human flesh can compress itself.

A good first-night audience, the conductor judged. Distinguished musicians and critics could be counted here in dozens; you could have assembled from among them, for your amusement, the professorial roster of an academy of music. A good audience indeed; it wasn't everywhere you'd find one so well educated musically. And surely nowhere else did the listeners look forward with such hungry longing to the first notes of a *première*.

The constant movement of people in the doorway had ceased; no one was entering now, but the doors still remained open, for even those left outside wanted to hear. It was time to begin.

The conductor turned to his company. Every man was in his place. But Schächter still did not give the signal: he was too deeply agitated, he had first to calm himself. With pride he surveyed the serried ranks of his gigantic choir, cast his glance over the mass of the orchestra, and fixed his eyes on the bench of soloists. He looked into their excited and shining eyes, caressed and encouraged each one with a glance. This is the end of our long preparations. We've done it! Now, together, we'll do our best to capture our audience and create a work no one shall ever forget.

He took up his baton. The auditorium fell silent. A strange, a special silence, unusual in the camp. Not the silence of bare walls and secret dread. The silence of quivering expectation. The silence of the lover anticipating the first caress.

Almost imperceptibly the baton moved. Almost inaudibly the first notes of Verdi's Requiem stole through the hall.

Schächter could remember the exact moment when he resolved to embark on the study of Verdi's Requiem. For a long time the idea had been provoking and luring him. To show up the mendacity of perverted ideas of pure and impure blood, of superior and inferior races, to expose them precisely in a Jewish camp, and precisely through the medium of art, in the field where a man's true worth can best be recognized. He wanted to bring together the most diverse group possible, and then let all men come and hear what art could be achieved by such a human mixture.

And in Verdi's Requiem, and no other work. Italian music with a Latin text, Catholic prayers, Jewish singers, and musicians from Bohemia, Austria, Germany, Holland, and Denmark, many even from Poland and Hungary. A Requiem studied and directed by an unbeliever, a Requiem in the ghetto. What a conception!

A splendid conception, and it gave him no rest, drawing him more irresistibly every day. What the Nazis had intended to make of the Terezín ghetto, what they still had in mind for it, he did not understand; no one of sound mind could understand it. But in one thing they had succeeded perfectly. They had assembled in one camp the greatest Jewish artists from a large part of Europe; and they had created conditions that force men to ponder deeply the fundamental questions of life and death.

It was precisely here, in the ghetto of Terezín, that he ought to study the Requiem; Schächter realized this ever more clearly. Perhaps never again would he have such an opportunity.

12

Where else would he be able to select thus, without limitation and according to his own artistic taste, from a great glut of outstanding and accomplished musicians; where else would he find such a sensitive and appreciative audience? Here everyone hungered and thirsted after art, longed feverishly for every tremor of deep human feeling, all the more passionately and fervently as the world in which they had been forcibly imprisoned became more unthinkably repulsive and barbarous. Here a conductor would not be hampered by jealousy and the changing whims of spoiled prima donnas; every artist would be glad and grateful for the last place in the choir. Nor would any concert agency attempt to instruct him in what the public likes and dislikes. Here he could create a work whose artistic limitations would be fixed only by the quality of the conductor himself.

He must study the Requiem here, he told himself. Probably the Germans would not even permit him to attempt Bach, Handel, or Mozart; moreover, that would be purely religious music, lacking this elemental ferocity. No, it must be Verdi and none other. But what would the prayer for the dead mean to prisoners in a concentration camp? Would it offer comfort or strength? And for whom were prisoners to pray?

For the dead, or perhaps also for those thousands who had vanished, borne away by the transports? A profound question. Schächter hoped that in the music he might find the solution, and he tried to quicken the spirit and warm to remembered life the eloquence of the notes. But he did not succeed; there was still something missing, something important, something decisive.

Until one day . . .

The unforgettable day when Schächter met the old beggar. Did it really happen, or had some feverish dream merely conjured up for him an old, remembered fairytale? How in the ancient days, when St. Peter or even the Lord God Himself— No, it was a beggar, a real old man of Terezîn, the counterpart of many a one to be found begging at any of the camp kitchens. He stood there in the row of bent old creatures and made his plea quietly and humbly.

"Nimmt der Herr die Suppe?" ("Does the gentleman want his soup?")

No, the gentleman didn't want it, that dingy, tasteless broth; he had no appetite for lukewarm water flavored with rotting turnips. Hey, cook, you can pour my share into this hungry old man's bowl.

That was how they met. But for a moment the beggar did not even mention his name; perhaps he was ashamed to reveal it. He might have been German or Italian or French or English; he spoke all languages fluently, as perhaps, after all, only St. Peter, or even— They fell into conversation; the old man asked eager questions about everything, and they soon got on to music, and thence to the Requiem.

"You fool," the old fellow shouted in the aggressively loud tones of one very hard of hearing, "have you any conception of what you've taken on? Study Verdi's Requiem here, in a concentration camp? Just try adding it up! Four soloists, and not the sort you'll find anywhere. Then one choir isn't enough, you've got to have two, otherwise you'll never manage the *Sanctus* fugue. Forty singers is nothing like enough, you must have eighty, and even that's very few, it should be at least a hundred and twenty. In London they once performed it with ten times that number. And what about the orchestra? That means at least sixty more people, and if you want to make do with a piano, it's no use thinking two hands are enough for the job, you'll need two pianos. But all that's not so important: in music you can always improvise, and better a small and perfect instrument than a colossal flop. The really fundamental problem lies in something quite different. You understand me?" yelled the old man excitedly. "In something quite different!"

You're a fine one, Schächter thought to himself. When you were begging for my soup, you did it pianissimo, you'd learned that all right. Now you're bellowing at me as though I were the deaf one.

But the old fellow noticed nothing amiss; he was roused and he could not be silenced.

"A Jew and a requiem—brrrr!" He shivered to the marrow of his bones. "Don't mistake me, it isn't the Jew that bothers me, it's the requiem. They don't go together at all. Not even a Protestant can study a requiem properly, let alone a Jew. You've got to be a Catholic for that, and a deeply devout Catholic, too! Believe me, believe me," he blurted wildly at Schächter, "this doesn't depend on art but on faith. A Jew can never properly understand the Requiem. Your Jew's a fool. He believes in a better life here on earth, he expects a just reward and just punishment here in this life, and if he can't attain justice, then he believes, incorrigible optimist that he is, that his son will attain it, or his

grandson, or at least his great-grandson. But
always here on earth, among the living. And
your Catholic is a still greater fool: he hopes for
final justice in another world. He consoles himself with the thought that someday the time will
come when all men will rise from the dead and
parade before the judgment seat of God. And
that Catholic melody of his has a quite specific
counterpoint, and they call it hell! How can a
Jew set out to perform the Requiem when he's
never gone in fear of hell and never believed in
it? When it's never even occurred to him to
imagine such a thing as the kingdom of the
devil?"

And that was the moment when Schächter
realized what it was that he had never yet been
able to grasp. The old man was right, but after
his own fashion, of course; old people still think
in their old ways, they don't see today, they're
living in the past and see things as they used to
be. But today a man can imagine the torments
of the damned better than Dante ever could,
and a Jew writhing in the talons of the Nazis
knows hell in all its horror, here among the
living. Moreover, the Requiem he would study
here must not be a Christian requiem; that
would not help or strengthen anyone in this

place. It must be a new, a different kind of requiem, with a fanatical faith in historical justice here in this world. Only such a requiem could they sing here in a concentration camp; only such music would prisoners comprehend, Jews, Christians, and unbelievers alike. He would perform for them a requiem that had never yet been heard.

The first soloist he chose for his cast was Francis. He came from Galicia, the son of a Jewish cantor, the grandson and great-grandson of cantors; his family had been singing since time immemorial. Praise be to the Jewish religious rituals, which cannot be solemnized without a tenor; thanks to them, you find plenty of good tenors among the Jews. Not, of course, vocalists celebrated for their high C's and their great arias, not heroic figures with shining armor and big bellies . . . Modest and ordinary enough singers outwardly, they sing touchingly of the small joys and the great sorrow of our life. And they lift up their warm, moving voices only in praise of the Lord. That was the kind of voice he was looking for.

Francis was a young fellow, an orphan, who had begun to study music in Vienna and fled before Hitler to Prague. He could have gone on farther by illegal transport, but they refused to take along his sister, a young girl of fifteen who was fragile and ailing. So they remained in Prague, and waited helplessly until the Hitlerite claws closed on them. They had been among the first to come to Terezín and worked on the farm. Every evening, in the barracks block, Francis sang Jewish songs to his comrades, and that was where Schächter had first heard him. He began to rehearse with him, first correct pronunciation, sound by sound. The ear of a Jewish cantor finds it hard to get accustomed to the open speech of Latin. But Francis was quick to learn, and soon not even a priest would have recognized in him a Jewish cantor.

Then he found his soprano, a voice as delicately controlled as the enchanting music of a carillon. She seemed still a virginal girl, so slender she was and so white. A fairy from a childhood story. A woman sent by fate; he knew it as soon as he set eyes on her.

"What's your name?" he asked her wonderingly when they brought her to him. A silly question! What could her name be—the child of Jewish parents born in Bavaria? Annemarie. He transformed it into Maruška, perhaps perversely, for the very reason that such a name suited her so badly. But he grew used to it, and everybody called her by it.

He was long in selecting the singer to whom he would entrust the mezzo-soprano part, until his brother, a violinist, called his attention to Elizabeth. They had just brought her into the ghetto; she took care of the littlest ones, and every evening the children gathered round her to hear her sing. With her alone he had no need to practice, for she was a singer of the first rank, and had sung many times in Verdi's Requiem. Where? She waved the question away. Why remember? She would be glad to sing, very glad; she had only one request. She had a husband, whom she wheeled about in a two-wheeled cart, for he was disabled, a reminder of the "the night of broken glass." "They didn't dare touch me at that time," she recalled sadly. "I was famous and popular." They had taken out their spite on her husband, who had been brought home to her out of the street crippled. He loved and understood music; there might even be times when he could give good advice. Could she bring him to rehearsals? She had friends who would carry him down into the cellar for her, and he'd have his own chair there; he wouldn't be any trouble to anyone.

And so Schächter gained, along with Elizabeth, his first listener. By that time he had also the embryo of an orchestra and a small choir, but he had not yet found his bass singer, and he continued the search vainly. Others were helping him in the hunt. Often they brought singers to him; he began to rehearse with several of them, only to end by adding them to his choir. None of them satisfied him in the solo part. They failed to qualify at the "receiving center," as Elizabeth's crippled husband called it.

"There's just one verse you must sing well for Schächter," he said in good-natured encouragement to every new candidate, "and he'll give you the solo part." But it was just that single chosen verse, it seemed, that no one could succeed in singing as Schächter wanted it.

"Don't worry about it so," Elizabeth comforted the unhappy conductor after every failure. "I've heard the Requiem many times with outstanding singers and *I* don't know which one you'd have chosen."

So, for the time being, Schächter did not fill the bass role; he made use of a stand-in. But meanwhile he did not waste time; he diligently rehearsed those parts where he already had the means to attempt a first version of the work.

" *'Dies irae, dies illa, solvet saeclum in favilla.'* Four times in the Requiem this verse is repeated, and always it brings a return to full harmony," Schächter explained, and the choir and instrumentalists listened to him attentively. "Four times this verse flames out as though from the depths of the abyss of inevitable fate, and only full chorus and orchestra could find a fitting means of artistic expression. Here there's no place for soloists, for individuals. For the day about which we're singing is the day of judgment of all men, and hangs over all men. Over all those who ravish and enslave and humiliate and rob and murder. This is no German *'der Tag,'* no day of arrogance, not even a day of victory or defeat. It is the day of wrath, of righteous wrath. The day in which the German *Wehrmacht*, torn to shreds, will moan and bleed under the shattering blows of the Red Army, when the very earth of Germany will crack and burst into flame and smoke and the thunder of thousands of exploding bombs. This is the *'dies irae'* of which we shall be thinking when we strike the kettle drums and launch from our throats the yell of the pursuing demons. Not for revenge, not to balance our own accounts, only for the cause of human justice."

Schächter had already succeeded in re-creating one great work in Terezín. He had produced Smetana's *Bartered Bride*—in a concert version, it's true, with piano, soloists, and chorus, but opera in a concentration camp had impressed the prisoners as something miraculous. With one stroke, Raphael Schächter had become the hero of the Terezín ghetto. He did not have to look for artists now; they came looking for him. So, to the study of this further work, he did not come unprepared. He even had a place where he could rehearse without interference, a great underground cellar allotted to him by the Jewish elder himself. Schächter had fixed it up to his own taste as a rehearsal room. For the production of the Requiem, he needed first of all sheet music and instruments.

The score he soon obtained; the Terezín police themselves smuggled it in to him and brought some music paper into the bargain, so that the individual parts could be copied out more easily. The instruments presented more of a problem. Outside the ghetto it was forbidden for Jews to possess such things; they had had to give them up to the German Reich, or so they had been ordered to do by the Reichsprotektor. But in the ghetto, anyone could have them, for the Camp Commandant of Terezín had permitted it. So it was necessary to obtain instruments outside and then smuggle them into the ghetto. A difficult and dangerous task. Perhaps never before had musical instruments been assembled at such a cost.

"Lunatics!" said the many who were doubtful. "They're risking their lives and they'll pay for it, you'll see, those here in the ghetto and those outside." But, strange to say, there are always people to be found who are willing to stake their lives for the sake of a thrill. And some too who will do as much for art.

The first instrument, a cello, was smuggled into the ghetto by Meisl. His friends from the

24

Prague orchestra had secretly brought it for him and hidden it in a deserted barn in the fields, and from there Meisl himself had brought it in on a cart, in a bundle of hay, impudently and therefore quite safely, even with some assistance from the SS. A few violins and violas had been brought by old Jews from Germany, for there they had not been forced to give up their instruments. A battered and apparently superfluous piano had been left in Terezín by its former owner; perhaps it would not have been worth his while to pay the freight on it. In the church of Terezín stood an intact harmonium, and Schächter had it brought into his rehearsal room; at practice it filled in for the missing voices and instruments. Then some workers, excavating in the cellars, dug up a rare treasure. In the labyrinthine passages of the Terezín ramparts they uncovered a walled-up hiding place and found in it, carefully wrapped and packed, the instruments of a military band: brass, woodwinds, and, in particular, a big drum and kettle drums. Finally, a certain foreman laborer from a group of Jews who traveled with an SS driver to unload wagons at the railway station of Bohušovice bet that he could smuggle a double bass into the ghetto. If that fellow manages it, Schächter said to himself, then I shall produce the Requiem.

It was no light matter, this of the double bass; something had to be done about it. It had already been lying in hiding for some weeks in Bohušovice at the house of a messenger who sometimes transported various goods for the Terezín Command. In doing so, he sometimes smuggled small things into the ghetto, but he could not think of a way to get the double bass in there. "I've got to learn to play the bass fiddle now," he lamented unhappily. "What would I say to the SS if they decided to search my house and found the thing there?" Then they brought another bass to him from outside, and immediately after that a third, and that made him exceedingly uneasy. "I'll light the stove with 'em," he threatened quite seriously. "Get 'em out of here!"

So he was glad when one of the Jewish foremen offered to help him get rid of them. It happened on the very evening when they had delivered several wagons of coal and two trucks full of "curios" at the railway siding of Bohu- šovice. Sometimes they brought here weird and wonderful goods from Germany; in particular, the authorities of the German Reich had decreed that everything from the commandeered Jewish property that could not be made use of in any other way should be sent to Terezín. So into the ghetto came hearses, prayer books, tailors' dummies, mustache nets, and other such important requisites. These two cars were full of boxes carefully and meticulously stacked, and in every box was placed reverently a gentleman's top hat. Truly historical wagons, bright with the whole luster of German Jewry from the old imperial days.

When the SS man laid eyes on this splendor, he nearly split his sides laughing, and he had to wash down so glorious a joke in appropriate fashion. Then the top hats took over the whole railway station. They played football with top hats that night, and for a Jew to have walked along the siding of Bohušovice without a top hat on his head would have been to risk his life—far more dangerous, in fact, than to vanish completely from the darkened siding for a while. And the SS man was not at all surprised when they found a bass viol in the wagon behind the hat boxes. On the contrary, that was just what had been missing. He immediately called off the working party from the coal, mustered a choir from among the dirty, top-hatted Jews, and ordered them to play and sing. And play and sing they did. All that was necessary was to strum on the open strings and sing whatever came to mind; and the SS man liked "There Goes Marina" best.

They brought a variety of goods into the ghetto that night—coal, top hats, and a good many other commodities in the top hats, notably smoked meats, all borne in procession by a top-hatted choir. The police at the gate of the ghetto couldn't get over their astonishment at the sight. And while "Marina" went again and again to the cemetery, the SS man, with great ceremony, escorted all three bass viols into the ghetto.

Patiently, with dedicated purpose and savage obstinacy, Schächter acquired what he needed for his Requiem. He already had sheet music, the majority of the instruments, a rehearsal room, and the possibility of selecting among the wealth of singers and instrumentalists. The more the study of the work deepened for him, the more often did he remember the old beggar.

That loud-voiced old man had been right: he could not manage with forty singers in his choir; even eighty was inadequate; there ought to be at least a hundred and twenty. But for the time being he would have been happy if he could have had the eighty. Where was he to get them so suddenly? There were plenty of enthusiastic and musically accomplished amateurs in Terezín, but first it was necessary to test them all gradually, to amass a great number of tested singers and then choose the best of them for the Requiem.

For that purpose he began to study more operas; in addition to *The Bartered Bride*, he took up *The Kiss* and after that *The Marriage of Figaro* and *The Magic Flute*, and for every one he acquired new singers as soloists and chorus, and all of them he drafted into rehearsals for the Requiem.

"You'll get a solo part in the opera," he tempted some artist of world reputation, "but in the Requiem you must sing in the choir for me." And when some of them recalled their former successes and wanted the solo part, he would say, "For opera many are called, but for the Requiem few are chosen."

He went to see other conductors, most of

them Germans and Austrians, and constantly urged them to begin the study of operas. "But I shan't give you my singers," he said. "You have plenty of friends and acquaintances: you must find and train your own singers and then lend them to me for the Requiem." And this example had its effect, for Klein, from his school in the garret, began to work on *Rigoletto*, *Tosca*, and *Carmen*, and Fisher made some first attempts upon the oratorio *Elijah*, and later *The Creation*. They formed orchestras and string quartets, and everywhere Schächter helped, and everywhere he took what he could find. It was exhausting work for him: every transport leaving the ghetto took artists away from him; every transport arriving brought him new ones.

In spite of all obstacles, the work grew, and with it grew the roster of his artists; the hall in the cellar was no longer big enough to hold them all. He worked out a considered and ingenious plan of rehearsals, and adhered to it strictly. He tried out all manner of combinations, so that voices and instruments should be pure, well rehearsed, and justly balanced over his whole company. And constantly he compared and selected among his singers and musicians, until some of his friends reproached him for it. In answer, he said, "A requiem is no mere pastime for any composer. Every one of them sets out to leave in his requiem his most precious legacy. And that places a heavy responsibility upon the conductor."

He was quite implacable about the selection of his soloists. No celebrated name could sway him; he knew what kind of voice he was looking for, and he would have no other. Three solo parts were already filled; only the fourth, the bass, was still missing. And without him it was no longer possible to proceed further with the rehearsals.

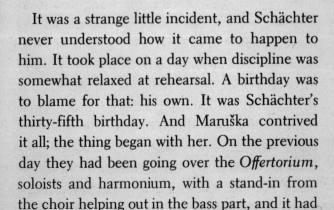

It was a strange little incident, and Schächter never understood how it came to happen to him. It took place on a day when discipline was somewhat relaxed at rehearsal. A birthday was to blame for that: his own. It was Schächter's thirty-fifth birthday. And Maruška contrived it all; the thing began with her. On the previous day they had been going over the *Offertorium*, soloists and harmonium, with a stand-in from the choir helping out in the bass part, and it had gone better than they had expected. But then they came to the seventieth bar, and Schächter broke off the rehearsal. There was something he didn't understand, he said, and he would need to think it over seriously. "Come tomorrow," he asked them. "I'm rehearsing with the choir, but with you I just want to repeat a few short bars: we'll soon get that over."

And so they met the next day in the cellar, soloists and choir together, not forgetting constant audience, Elizabeth's husband. Schächter came into the room surly and ill-tempered, not even remembering that it was his birthday.

"Damn it!" he swore in the doorway, and slapped the score down upon a chair. Then he called the singers to him at the harmonium, opened the score, pointed out certain bars, and began to get excited again. "Just look here"—he appealed to them as witnesses—"look what we've got here in the *Offertorium*. 'Beware, O man,' says the Latin text, 'that you don't fall straight into the Lion's maw, into the darkness of the pit of hell.' And suddenly"—Schächter pointed a finger somewhat more cheerfully into the score—"however it got there, there it is!—notice how Verdi changes the mood in one bar—suddenly Michael appears, Michael, who has the high command as standard bearer in the heavenly host, to point the trembling souls safely on their way and lead them away from the dark horrors into the radiance of the light of heaven.

"Well, and now let's see what the music has to say. We've made a mess of things, it laments at the beginning, we're in it up to the neck, it looks bad for us. And then, all in a fraction of a second! You see? Here's the change, in the sixty-second bar, just on this syllable 'but.' That little Latin 'sed' has become for us the touchstone of art. And here it isn't at all little, and that's the whole trouble. I've been knocking my brains out over it ever since yesterday. It's confoundedly long, it trails its way through seven whole bars, like stretched chewing gum, but the demands it makes! It's the watershed between stinking hell and blissful heaven, and at the same time it must serve as a heraldic fanfare for an archangel, announcing the approach of a personage as exalted as the standard bearer Michael. Damn it! If only Verdi had chosen some syllable with 'o' or 'u,' something magical could be made of it, but what can we do with 'sed'?"

They began the rehearsal, first from bar thirty-one, then from bar forty-seven, Schächter at the harmonium writhing like a ballet dancer and trying his best to improve on that unfortunate "*sed*" with his accompaniment, but all in vain: he could not get past that seventieth bar. He called a halt and sat down apart from the others, not even noticing how they had their heads together over something. He was angry. With Verdi. Such an outstanding musician, and at this critical point he chose to make use of a bloodless, miserable monosyllable that could only be bleated or whined, what else?

And suddenly his mind and his sky cleared. They were forgetting to pronounce in the Italian manner. Italian women would sing that confounded "*sed*" more like "seed," and with such a lengthened "eee" sound that it was possible to shrill a wholly fitting salute.

"I've got it!" Schächter cried, and hustled his soloists to their places. And at once they began.

From the first, everything went fairly satisfactorily; even that unlucky "*sed*" in its new form sounded quite acceptable to him on its very first hearing. But suddenly he had the stupefying impression that his soprano had snapped "rrraff" at him like a dog barking, and immediately they all pounced upon him like a pack of hounds. For Maruška, solo, had sung "Raphael" instead of "Michael," and all the other singers had joined their voices to hers. "Vivat Raphael!" they cried. Here you are, Raphael, our standard bearer, they were telling him, for your comfort here's our birthday present to you.

He could not be angry with them, but for that day discipline had broken down in the whole company, and that was a thing that had never happened to him before. He began to rehearse the Sanctus, first with one choir. The soloists remained, being curious to see how the singers would succeed with the fugue for two choirs. And when the whole room was quivering with the proclamation of glory, and heaven and earth already filled with it, at that moment—an unheard-of and unexpected thing—an alien voice interrupted the rehearsal.

"Please, please, do that passage just once more," begged Elizabeth's husband in a trembling voice.

They stood aghast. Unheard of, to interrupt like that. What had come over him? Schächter controlled himself quickly; there was nothing he could refuse their cripple. "We'll repeat the *Sanctus* again from the beginning," he ordered the choirs, and they began again. " '*Sanctus, sanctus*,' " boomed the basses. But the singers got no further, for there was a new interruption.

"Please, that man there"—Elizabeth's husband pointed excitedly among the singers in the choir—"no, not him, the next, the one beside him . . ."

Out of the ranks stepped a tall, thin man, perhaps forty years old but already very gray. They all knew him, a modest, taciturn soul named Josef.

"Don't be angry," pleaded the anxious voice from the corner, "but please let's try Josef with Elizabeth."

After three weeks, Josef came to the "reception center." And when the words "*Confutatis maledictis, flammis acribus addictis*" vibrated menacingly through the rehearsal room, Schächter, too, realized that he had found his bass soloist. But he never fully understood how such a thing could happen to him, that it was not he who had chosen Josef but their silent, self-effacing listener.

And thus to Elizabeth and Francis he added

the last soloist, Josef, and that same day gave birth to the nickname "Their Majesties."

On only one occasion did Schächter come last to rehearsal. They were already waiting impatiently for him, afraid that something had happened to him. And then suddenly he erupted among them, loud, talkative, a changed man, shouting from the doorway that there wouldn't be a rehearsal. And yet he climbed to his place, seized his baton, and rapped on the music stand.

"Come close, please, everybody here to me, I've got great news for you," he proclaimed in a ceremonious voice that quivered with emotion, and looked down upon them joyfully. "The Command has decreed," he cried exultantly, "that the artists of Terezín will no longer be sent to the transports, they'll remain here in Terezín. They're saved! The Jewish chief elder has registered our entire company among the artists. I've just handed over to him the list of names."

And he jumped down from his dais among his

astonished, bewildered soloists and musicians and embraced them one after another. Think of it! This is salvation for us, for your wives and children, the end of terrors. The war must end soon now. The concentration camps will be thrown open. The Germans have lost, the Nazis have lost, already they're looking around desperately for an alibi, they must have things weighing heavily on their consciences now if they're sparing Jewish artists. Who would ever have thought of such a reversal, the Hitlerites sparing Jewish artists!

The people in the cellar began to grasp it at last and suddenly they had no idea what to do; everyone was laughing and weeping. Raphael was right; the war had ended for them. They had escaped! By a hair, but they had escaped. They were saved!

Slowly and carefully Schächter made his way through to his dais again and mounted it, but no one took any notice; they were still embracing and kissing one another. It was not possible to understand or savor such news all in a moment. Nor did Schächter wish to interrupt anyone in his outburst of joy; he only stood and looked around him with shining eyes, proudly, victoriously.

Yes, they would be victorious; he believed it now, he no longer doubted. And no one had believed in him, not even that ironical mocker within him, that other, rational "I." You've lost your mind, Raphael, it had nagged him; who ever heard of such a thing as producing Verdi's Requiem in a Jewish concentration camp? You're a dreamer, a fool. No one had believed in him, not even his singers; what mattered to them was not the work but the rehearsals, calling up, as they did, memories of better days, helping them to forget, giving them strength and hope. It was that they had all understood, and for that they had been grateful. But no one had believed that he would complete the work.

True, he had set himself a tremendous goal, but life would have neither charm nor value if man were not battling his way toward such a goal. And he would achieve his end, now he believed it. In a Jewish concentration camp he would produce Verdi's Requiem. He would assemble whatever he needed for the work. He would train a masterful company—if need be, even his hundred and twenty singers and great orchestra—and create a work whose artistic limitations would be fixed only by the limits of the conductor's art.

The soft, constant tapping of his baton slowly calmed their excited minds. They got control of themselves, and each one went back to his place. They quite understood. There would be no rehearsal that day, but they would sing something, joyfully, from their hearts; they could not go away thus silently and without a sign; somehow they must close this happy day with a fitting celebration.

"At one point the Requiem reminds us of that ancient and solemn promise given to Abraham and his seed," said Schächter with a smile. "And we'll sing it now, and we can shout our loudest, so that they'll hear us even in the solitude of heaven. Yes, we'll shout aloud in the ear of the Lord God, 'See what they're doing in this world to the seed of Abraham, is it nothing to you? Have you not forgotten what you promised?' We may well ask that, since they've marked us so clearly as Jewish stock—don't you think so?" said Schächter, grinning at his soloists; but he fell back suddenly into deep thought. "The *Offertorium* ends with the words '*De morte transire ad vitam*,' " he said gravely. "Yes, we'll sing that, we'll believe that for us too the gate of the concentration camp will open, and together we shall step out into a new and better life.

"Now, then," he concluded merrily again, "find the *Offertorium*, bar eighty-nine. The bass begins, and in the orchestra the bassoon— '*Quam olim Abrahae!*' "

They're going!

No one cried out the fatal words, no one even whispered them, yet somehow everyone knew. Even here beneath the earth, in the deep cellar of the Terezín barracks. They penetrated into the brain, permeated the body, saturated the blood. They paralyzed the nerves, constricted the breath, froze the flesh.

The hand above the conductor's rostrum never moved. Poised, as though turned to stone in an unfinished motion, it pointed into emptiness, aimlessly, thoughtlessly. After a moment it contorted in a ragged movement and sank feebly. The only movement in the long, twilit room.

The silence had penetrated here, Schächter realized, from outside, from above, from everywhere, and now it spread throughout the room, strident and imperative, it overwhelmed everything, froze the walls into dumbness, maimed the people; not even a quiver of air moved here now. The murmur is silenced, the hum of everyday life, which at other times flows everywhere, in the streets, in the house, even in you yourself, though solitary. The walls receive it and return an echo, the air is tremulous and warm with it, there is so much of it everywhere, and yet you never notice it. As you never feel the air you breathe. It's a part of life.

And suddenly the hum has ceased. At first you don't even realize that something has happened. There is only a chill somewhere in the marrow of your bones, as though the coldness of the dark night had touched you. As though the breath of death itself had wafted over you. Your body stiffens, your nerves drum out an alarm, something is happening, something has hold of you, something is approaching. Something fatal and dreadful; it's coming, it must come, you cannot turn it back, you can only wait helplessly.

Then suddenly you are aware of the silence. And you understand it. *They're going!* it cries. They're going, your quivering nerves clamor. *They're going*, whistles your constricted breath.

In the deep, wide cellar nothing moved;

everything seemed devoid of life. Only the conductor's tired gaze slid fluidly from place to place. It did not halt on the motionless seated figures or see the deeply bowed heads. Only spiritlessly it noted the gaps in the rows; to these it was drawn. In all those places there were once people, friends, singers. Now there were only empty seats. A shattered, dismembered choir.

Right at the front was the soloists' bench. A woman sat there, horror eloquent in her dilated eyes. Schächter was trembling. Maruška! At least she was left to him, she, the most precious. A broad forehead, unmarked by wrinkles. No one would ever realize all that she had suffered; only her eyes were always eloquent, seeing, sorrowing eyes. Now she shrank and crouched there before him, as though oppressed from all sides by the pitiless pressure of emptiness. Beside her—void places. Only yesterday the others had sat there, Francis, Josef, and Elizabeth. Their Majesties, as he himself had nicknamed them; "the Hapsburgs," the choir had called them. Without mockery, in a friendly spirit, only because of the accidental harmony of their names, so droll, and in a concentration camp so uplifting. Yes, only yesterday they were all here. And now?

Through the narrow chinks of the cellar loop holes, pierced through the wall close to the ceiling, into the depths of the cellar fell the sound of weary, shuffling footsteps. There above them, almost within reach of their hands, nailed boots rang on the pavement of the Terezín street. How well they knew the look of those departing! How they tramped in great crowds through the empty streets of the ghetto, their wives and children beside them, staring mutely at the closed windows of houses and barracks blocks. How winter and summer alike they went bundled and swaddled in warm underclothing, with winter suits and long coats, reeling and bent beneath the weight of great bundles and rucksacks. Thus they were passing now, Francis with his sister, Josef with his old mother. And down to the transport, Elizabeth was trundling her maimed and weakening husband on his cart.

They had betrayed him, Schächter thought, boiling with rage, they had all betrayed him. They could have stayed here; they had only to let their families depart alone. But people have no sense when the heart commands, when the blood calls. All his reproaches and arguments had been in vain; they had not even allowed him to speak. They had failed him, left him here with his shattered company and his unfinished work; maybe they'd never really believed that he would succeed in completing it, when he had come to shipwreck so often. And now, for the sake of their families, they were sacrificing everything, even themselves, and their sacrifice was itself in vain; the help they could give to the others would be little enough.

Petr, the bassoon player, had had to go. Schächter couldn't hold it against him; the man couldn't forsake his wife and children. Nor had the others really had any choice: twelve from the orchestra, twenty-three singers from the choir. There was no way of helping even Meisl. Poor Meisl, the cellist, the first to smuggle a musical instrument into the ghetto. "I had to take the risk," he always used to say. "How else could I have kept four little children?" And now both Meisl and his children were off to the transport, and only the cello still lay here; he could not hope to smuggle it any further.

Schächter wiped his streaming face with his hand. A deep and heavy sigh quivered through the cellar, as though people there were awaking from a feverish, suffocating sleep.

They would not sing now. They couldn't now,

when outside, almost within touch, men and women and children were trudging toward the cattle wagons and setting out on a journey to an unknown and dreadful goal.

They couldn't sing now; even Schächter recognized it. And yet, like a sleepwalker, blindly obedient to some subconscious command, slowly he took up his baton.

"We will continue the rehearsal," he said in a constricted voice, "we mustn't stop now. We'll begin again from the beginning, first the part without soloists."

And after a moment he added quietly, "We'll begin with the verse: '*Requiem aeternam dona eis, Domine, et lux perpetua luceat eis.*' This verse will always recall to us the footsteps we have just heard pass by above us. And in these words we express what we feel so deeply this day:

" 'Rest and peace grant unto them, O Lord, on their onward journey, grant them strength and purpose, and never take away hope from them!' "

The last ranks of the transport had passed by the barracks. The echo of heavy footfalls had stilled into silence, and with it the song of the choir also fell silent, that last message to those departing. Everywhere the murmur of everyday life trembled again. Only in the depths of the cellar was it still quiet; no one had a word to say. Schächter, too, was silent; he dismissed them with a confused motion of his hand. Run home: that's the end of rehearsal for today. The singers hesitated, approaching their conductor doubtfully, but he repelled them; no, he was not going yet, he was staying on here for a while. They understood him, and went silently away. Schächter was left alone in the rehearsal room.

How could it happen, he asked himself over and over again, such a reversal! Only a week ago they were exulting and rejoicing, *"Quam olim Abrahae promisesti"*—"I shall complete my work," he had cried aloud. And today? He had a dismembered choir and orchestra; of his four soloists, only one remained to him. How could it have happened?

The Command had promised exemption for the artists; he himself had joyfully announced that news to them all. But of course the Command had also ordered that all small children, orphans, widows and widowers, cripples, blind people, and consumptives be drafted to the transports—in the interests of the inhabitants of the ghetto, they said, who would thereby be enabled to enjoy a better life. The Command always honors its promises. Could they help it if Francis' sister had fallen ill with tuberculosis in Terezín, and the mother of Meisl's children had died there? It was not their fault that Elizabeth's husband had come into Terezín already a cripple on a push cart. The Command fulfills its promises, but it also demands that its orders be respected; that's surely a fair exchange. It did not order Meisl or any of the other exempted artists to the transports; they came of their own will and enrolled themselves, and their request could hardly be refused. The Command doesn't behave inhumanly; it will not tear families apart.

A devilish plan, argued Schächter, and none of the ordinary killers and murderers thought it up, nobody from the SS, who kick and club and beat, none of these people here in Terezín, not even the Commandant, maybe not even Günther in Prague. It must have been one of those elegant, smooth, socially refined ornaments of the upper ranks, who behave even to Jews with punctilious politeness, and won't endure brutality. Heaven help the SS man who strikes a Jew in front of them. These are the real deceivers; the more unexceptionably they behave on the surface, the more dangerous they are. Eichmann could have devised this murderous plan, or Moese . . . Yes, it could well be Moese: he was drawn to art, and prided himself on his culture, and was pleased to have even Jewish artists presented to him; he might very well abuse art for his dirty purposes. With them everything is deception, lies and deceit. The organization of mass murder—that's something they can do well, they take pleasure in it, they feed on it. So how could they now pretend any attachment to man, to art? What can the Terezín Requiem matter to them? And yet he had been taken in once more, he had not seen through their villainy, for a while he had believed again. Hard not to believe, when you hope so desperately for salvation.

What now? Was he to let everything go, or begin all over again? How many times already had he begun again? How many of his people had been torn from him today, unfeelingly, inhumanly, barbarously? From the front row, from the soloists, three; and from the rest?

He stared at the empty benches, his gaze wandering despairingly from place to place. Only yesterday they all stood there, singing.

Suddenly his eye fell upon the cello; he had seen it earlier, but only now did he become aware of it. It struck a chill to his heart, Meisl's cello. Even you they've torn apart, the artist and his instrument. To you he used to confide his thoughts, through you he turned his love and joy into music, through you he lamented his pain, fear, and humiliation, you were his most intimate friend. And now you stand here mute, no one to fondle you, no one to caress you and warm you in his arms . . .

Schächter stepped down from his dais. He, too, would have liked to fondle it now, to forget for a moment, to confide his grief and his weakness. He drew near to the cello, he was reaching out his hand to it, when he faltered and stopped. He couldn't play, he couldn't now, he was trembling violently throughout his whole body, and in a moment more he was overwhelmed by a burst of desperate, convulsive weeping. Not for his ruined work, not for his shattered hopes; he wept bitterly now for Meisl's four children, behind whom the doors of the cattle wagons had closed today.

His weeping grew quieter and calmer, hushed into silence. He had control of himself now, he could consider calmly. He must not sit here wretched and irresolute beside Meisl's cello; he should take his stand at the conductor's rostrum, that was his place, from there he directed and made decisions. He would not give up, he would not retreat even now; he was so near to his goal, he would go on fighting. Somehow he would fill up the rows of his orchestra; the instruments still remained to him, and somehow he would find players for them. The choir, perhaps, need not give him so much trouble, for he had always rehearsed more singers than he had selected for the Requiem. He would attempt it with a smaller choir and orchestra—if need be, with piano only; somehow he would manage it.

And perhaps there was a mezzo-soprano he could have, he recalled suddenly. Also Elizabeth, but a different Elizabeth; he called her Betka or sometimes "church Betka." A country priest had taught her to sing; it did not trouble him at all that the solo in his church should be sung by a Jewess. A flexible, caressing voice, a rarity in a mezzo-soprano; and a heart of gold that girl must have, for even in Terezín she played the sister of mercy, there, where the work was hardest and the need of devotion greatest, in the closed cells among the old, lice-ridden madmen.

He would almost certainly have chosen her for the solo part in the first place if she had not made one bad slip. "You've got to be able to enunciate, girl, and enunciate properly," he had lectured her irritably that day. "You sang in Latin in church, yes, but that priest of yours taught you to pronounce Latin the Czech way." He could still hear his own voice delivering that hurtful homily. "Learn to pronounce the word '*lacrymosa*' properly," he had flashed out at her heedlessly, "and you needn't even sing that tearful sound, it sings itself. But for that you must get rid of those hard Czech head sounds. The first two syllables are only throwaways, background painting for that culminating 'mo.' '*La-cry-mo-sa*.' But you come bursting out like a runaway horse with the 'la,' and then that 'cry' of yours! What couldn't an Italian or even a French singer do with that soft 'r'! Plead, caress, confess her passion, laugh and mourn, everything she could make it do. But you? You open your throat and plump out a fine, lusty 'cry.' And the culminating 'mo' is no better. A Czech can only use the syllable 'o' for scolding and cursing, he knows no other but the open 'o,' worse luck! And then, you're a girl, the first word you think of is '*móda,*' and you pronounce your 'o' as if it was the fashions you were singing about—'-*mawww-da*'!"

And with that unhappy "*mawww-da*" he had quite crushed Betka that day; he had realized it at once himself. She had recoiled in some bitterness, though of course only for a short time, for she was the gentlest of souls, a mezzo-soprano and a heart of gold, most happy combination. He had not been fair to her. Perhaps he'd been in an irritable mood. Perhaps he'd already been counting on the other Elizabeth, for his brother had just told him about her; he knew her well from the old days, a singer of the first rank. He would not have to teach *her* how to pronounce Latin.

So "church Betka" went into the choir, having stumbled at the "reception center" over one single word: "*lacrymosa.*" But even when she was in the choir, he could never escape from the sound of her voice, so young and so fresh and yet unobtrusive, a voice remarkably controlled and balanced. A heart of gold and a mezzo-soprano! Constantly he found himself comparing the two Elizabeths. That country priest had known very well what he was doing when he let a Jewess sing the solos in his church.

He ought to try the same part with her again now, if she still wanted it and would not refuse him.

Very softly the cellar door opened a little. A friend? Maruška? Of course—Betka!

"Raphael, come, you mustn't lurk here in this dark hole by yourself. You haven't had anything to eat yet. Come along, I'm boiling some potatoes, I'll put some margarine with them and some dried onion—"

"Yes, I will come, Betka, I'll come gladly. But just have patience with me a moment, there's still something I would like to try again."

He went to the harmonium and hunted through the sheaves of music. He took out one part and silently offered it to Betka.

Lacrymosa.

"When we go home," Schächter used to say, "I'm going to write a short story. Or perhaps a fairy story. Yes, more likely a fairy story. About how hell moved up into heaven, and heaven found itself down in hell. Or: how Raphael got his tenor and bass easily and quickly."

He already had one tenor then, Rosenfeld, the finest singer in Terezín, but he could not rely on him, for he was already a sick man when he came into the ghetto, and he often fell ill, so it was imperative to have another one in reserve. But it was the bass that gave him the most trouble, as once before he had hunted for him laboriously until Elizabeth's husband had pointed his finger at Josef. But now indeed he did not know what to do to solve his difficulty, for the kind of bass voice he wanted was not to be found anywhere in Terezín.

"When we go home," repeated Schächter— and indeed he very often repeated those words—"the Jews must reform their religious ceremonial. Why should it be only a tenor who's allowed to sing in the rites? Next time they should divide things up evenly, half for the tenor and half for the bass. But of course," he reflected doubtfully, "that's if the congregation don't raise violent objection to such a church reform. The bass voice has always been the natural vehicle of the brood of hell: maybe they won't even let it into the temple."

He might joke about it as much as he liked, but he still could not find the right bass. He searched and asked; in the choir he had so many of them that he hardly knew what to do with them, but the right one simply would not be found. The time came when he thought of nothing else; sometimes he himself realized that he was becoming obsessed by the idea, and that damned voice pursued him at every step.

Until at last it even happened that in the open street he began to hear the distant echo of a marvelous voice. A bass, and what a bass! The authentic voice of the lord of hell. I'm hearing things, Schächter said sternly to himself, now I'm really going out of my mind. Moreover, the voice did not come from below, as was fitting, but from above, out of heaven. But, for all that, it brought a message from the infernal kingdom, for the moment it ceased, the street was veiled in thick smoke and stinking fumes.

"As if it were the devil himself!" Schächter stormed, and rushed into the nearest house. Oh, no, sir, they told him, there's no singer lives here. Maybe on the floor above. And thus Schächter came story by story to the attics, and then to the roof.

And he had made no mistake; hell had really

moved into heaven. On the roof, enwreathed in a cloud of smoke and soot, a dreadful black figure lashed a phenomenal tail. "A chimney sweep!" Schächter shouted loudly, by way of demonstrating, outwardly at least, that he was not afraid of the devil. "A singer!" thundered back the chimney sweep with the devil's voice.

A week later Schächter presented to his company his new discovery, his bass. In Terezín he worked as a chimney sweep, and his name was Charles. But they already had two Charleses in the company, so they called this one Mephistopheles.

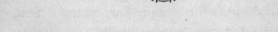

On the same day when Schächter presented his new bass soloist to the assembled singers, the tenor Rosenfeld did not come to rehearsal. He was ill again, delirious with fever, and they had had to take him away to the sick bay.

"We're out of luck, there's nothing to be done about it," Schächter repeated sadly. "Today we ought to have been complete at last. But Rosenfeld will soon be fit again," he consoled himself and the others. "I've been to the doctors, they're doing all they can, we shan't lose our tenor. From what I hear, things are worse with Hitler. They were saying in the hospital that there's no medicine much good for what ails him. And they must know what they're talking about at the hospital: they get all the latest reports. So here's today's great thought for you:

If Hitler's star's descended
Before our Requiem's ended,
Well—we won't be offended!

And now we'll begin with the *Sanctus* fugue: we don't need the tenor for that."

They finished the fugue and waited to see what their conductor would decide on next. But at that instant the door of the rehearsal room was hurled open and an unknown young man darted in among them. In the very doorway he stiffened in astonishment, and wonder flashed wildly over his frightened face. He was panting heavily, like a hunted beast, and in an instant he leaped forward again, without even closing the door properly behind him, and sprang into the orderly ranks of the singers. They had no time even to look at him fully; they noticed only the yellow star upon his jacket. They already knew what must happen next. They stood silent and motionless.

The door of the cellar was slowly pushed open, and an SS man peered cautiously inside. They knew him: Haindl. He had a heavy club in his hand. He leaned his back against the door and stared around the rehearsal room in astonishment.

"Sixty-nine Jews at rehearsal," Schächter reported loudly and clearly.

Haindl took no notice of him; his eyes were roving over every corner of the cellar, and slowly he swung his cudgel. He knew of this rehearsal room, but he had never entered it until now; he had been trailing one Jew, and now he had a whole host of them. He gazed suspiciously around him and said not a word, asked no questions. He strode into the room and silently prowled along the ranks of motionless prisoners, staring into faces, measuring figures; it was obvious he could not recognize the right one. Suddenly he laughed, confidently, cunningly.

"*Weitermachen!*" he shouted savagely. ("Go on with what you're doing!")

Schächter hastily considered how to begin, what to choose. Something loud, something tremendous, where the voice of an individual could be lost. In any case the SS man understood nothing about singing; it was quite possible to act out a convincing comedy for his benefit.

"We'll repeat the *Sanctus* fugue," he ordered, and stretched out his hand at once and gave the signal with his baton. " '*Sanctus, sanctus, sanctus,*' " pealed the choir, and Haindl strode along the rows of the singers, peering bewilderedly into their wide-open mouths. He could not distinguish who was singing properly and who was singing badly; he knew only—he could see for himself—that they were all singing.

But the conductor could distinguish. A voice he had never heard before in the choir, ravishingly full and sweet, without flaw, a tenor! The choir, too, heard the new voice and understood, and immediately their singing became more joyful and exultant. You from the SS, you're hardly the blessed one who cometh in the name of the Lord, but also you're no match for us, we've got you beaten. *Hosanna, hosanna* in the highest!

The SS man stormed out of the cellar scowling, not even waiting for the prescribed salute. No doubt he was now lurking behind the door to see whether the young Jew would betray himself. The rehearsal continued. The soloists came in to sing the *Agnus Dei*, then the *Lux Aeterna*, and when they reached the point where the tenor must come in, Schächter did not stop them but stretched out his baton toward the unknown, gave him a nod, and—wonder of wonders!—the young man began to sing the solo part.

" 'O angels, rejoice and be glad . . .' " How beautifully the boy sang. *Hosanna, hosanna*, Schächter exulted with him, and smiled blissfully, for now there was no one missing. Now at last he could continue in his work.

"He hunted me with his club all through the barracks, I could hear him sniffing on my heels. I thought for certain I would never shake him. And suddenly I heard singing. *Hosanna!* I thought to myself, he's shot me, that's what it is, and I'm blundering into heaven. But that was no go, either. The singing wasn't coming from above but from below, and I doubt if they sing '*Hosanna!*' in hell. And why should they be

singing Verdi in heaven, it went through my
head as I ran, they've surely got their own
special music there. I couldn't understand all
this, and I didn't have time to consider. Halluci-
nations most likely, I thought, I've gone out of
my mind with terror. But still I could hear the
singing, and it drew me. I thought there must be
safety there. Where they were singing like that,
they couldn't be bad people. So here I am. And
my name's Roderich."

The women of the choir had been listening
attentively to his story, deeply moved. They
shook their heads unbelievingly as they looked
at him, for it seemed to them that this wasn't
even possible. A young fellow like this, with
reddish-gold curls and great green eyes and a
straight, even slightly upturned nose, and he
was a Jew! He brought to life for them the
figures of the angels as Raphael and Murillo had
painted them; there was something boyish,
something of the urchin, in this mischievous
face. Even Schächter shook his head dubiously.
This story of heaven and hell he could
understand—he himself had lived through
something similar—but never yet had he heard
of a Jewish cantor giving his son the name
Roderich.

"Your father was a cantor?" he asked, and the boy replied at once that he had never known his father, he was illegitimate, but his mother had sung for thirty years in the chorus of the Vienna opera.

"And how did you come into the ghetto?"

That, of course, was a long story, and they were listening to it well into the evening, in a close circle in Schächter's garret under the roof.

The boy was a Catholic, a Roman Catholic, and his mother belonged to the same faith; he had not even known that he was of mixed blood, for she had never told him anything about his father. He had learned to sing when he was a very little boy (his mother naturally led him in that direction), and he had even sung in the Vienna Boys Choir. He was just sixteen years old when Hitler overpowered Austria. His mother wanted to get him across the frontier at all costs; her ideal had always been Italy, the land of song, and she had acquaintances everywhere there in the theaters. For money, much could be done in Italy. And she had some success. She got him false papers and gave him everything she had, money and jewels. There's going to be a world war, she said, people will be robbed of all their property, like last time. You learn to sing, that's something no one can take away from you.

And he was glad to get out of Vienna: the ground had been burning his heels there, it was getting a little too hot to hold him. Girls? What, at sixteen? Well . . . yes, something like that, but also he was looking forward to Italy, to the sea and the sun, to living with false papers. Everything about the adventure lured him. And things went very well for him—he had more luck than sense—until finally, when he was almost at his goal, this thing happened to him. In Milan. Of course, it's a strange story, really. Yes, there was a girl mixed up in it. They investigated him and, in the process, found out that by rights he was a German citizen. And they deported him back to Vienna, and there he was immediately clapped into military uniform.

And only then did his mother tell the whole truth. She produced old letters to prove that his father had been a Jew, a pure-blooded Jew; and a quarter share of Aryan blood was not enough to constitute Aryan origin. His mother had meant well: the ghetto of Terezín seemed safer to her than the Russian front for a boy of mixed blood. But he hadn't even known what his mother was planning behind his back. It was just a month ago that they suddenly withdrew him from the garrison, and he had no idea where the escort was taking him. In his soldier's uniform he came right into the ghetto, and only here, from the Jewish elder, did he get a full explanation of what had been happening to him. But he hadn't been able to tell him anything about his mother; they had imprisoned her in Vienna.

"And what was this affair of yours with Haindl? I suppose that's a strange story, too?"

"Haindl is a pig!" flamed Roderich. "He pesters Jewish girls. Jewish blood doesn't stink to him when it's girls. But this time he burned his fingers. I had a crack at him up in the attic, in the dark. He doesn't know who it was who shoved a fist under his jaw. And before he was off the floor, I was away. He didn't get a good look at me, so let him hunt and spy as much as he likes.

"To tell the truth, in the dark I didn't understand at once myself that it was an SS man in front of me," Roderich admitted, "or I might have thought twice, but it's happened now. It's happened and I don't regret it.

"But it was hell, plain hell," he said, breathing quickly again at the remembrance, "when he chased me from attic to cellar. And hell suddenly changed into paradise for me. Can you imagine what bliss it was, how it did my heart good, when I stood there yelling 'Hosanna!' straight into that stupid, furious face of his?"

They could indeed imagine it, and they took Roderich to their hearts. For his impudent angel's face and for this story of heaven and hell, they called him Cherubino.

Schächter had possessed himself of a new acquisition; he was boasting of him to all and sundry. He had a new constant listener. "My lucky pig," he used to say of him tenderly. "*Unser Mascotchen!*" Maruška lovingly called him. ("Our little mascot!") He was a man famous in the world of music, a scholar, critic, and historian, he had many degrees and honorary titles, and after one of them they began to speak of him as "our Court Councilor." Schächter had been looking for him for a long while around all the kitchens of Terezín, until suddenly, on opening night of *The Kiss*, he came and presented himself. Yes, it was he, that loud-voiced, hectoring, deaf old beggar who had helped him to grasp the significance of the Terezín Requiem. He rushed upon him with open arms, and Schächter embraced him at once. "Are you practicing the Requiem?" he asked eagerly, and immediately he began to coax and plead: "Take me to rehearsals!"

And Schächter took him, rather to show him off to them all than for any other reason, for he was proud of him. But the old man would not move from the cellar. They always found him there in the rehearsal room as often as they came there; perhaps he even slept there. And unceasingly he pored over the score. It was interesting to watch him as, hunched over the music, he frowned agitatedly or smiled blissfully. "This is my orchestra, and these are my ears," he would say, pointing to the score and then to his eyes.

After every rehearsal they gathered around him and began talking. Often they could not make out how he, almost deaf as he was, could grasp so many details.

"Those horns in the '*Tuba mirum*' ought to ring out more stridently—here, I'll show you where I mean," he once pointed out, and Schächter's first thought was that to a deaf man the horns might well sound more beautiful the louder they were played. But he tried it through in accordance with his advice, and the Court Councilor was plainly right.

On another occasion he said, "Today it went famously, only if I were you I would liven up the tempo more in the '*Rex tremendae.*' I'll sing you the part I mean." And sing he did on the spot, and though his singing was terrible, he expressed his meaning with face and lips and hands so intuitively that they saw at once what he was getting at.

They were rehearsing now every day, and in the most various combinations. Schächter had formed two small choirs and laid the foundations of two more; he had also selected a group that could play with a smaller orchestra, and had done his best to adapt the score for them. And constantly he polished and refined, nothing escaped him, he spared no one, and certainly not himself, he changed tempo, rhythm, and the emphasis of individual voices, he frowned and spluttered as he stressed and sharpened, and held his breath, pursed his lips, and half closed his eyes as he hushed and soothed.

"A listener would never dream," he often said, "how wonderful it is to cast a spell with music, when we change the tempo even imperceptibly, when we hush away the sound into quietness, or stress a certain instrument. Alter the rhythm and gradation by the least degree, and you can turn the prayer for the dead into a battle hymn."

"He's done enough spell-casting with us, why doesn't he go on to the final rehearsals?" the singers sometimes demanded, and appealed to their Court Councilor for support.

"Everyone must take his part right into his blood. Only when that's done can the conductor attempt a final version of the work," the old man soothed them, and at once began to enlarge ardently: "Art is no light matter. Every conductor must have several 'I's,' several identities. One, the director, hears every voice and every instrument, and must be in full control of them every moment, able to impress upon this large assembly of performers and instruments his own conception. But he must do more, as though he had several brains, as though he could think simultaneously in the most varying spatial dimensions and in every one independently, securely, and consciously. He is also the listener, he must be: music calls up in him memories, moods, and he again pours into it his own longings and hopes, his fears, joys, and sorrows. Even every one of you must think with several brains, experiencing the emotion of the listener and at the same time watchfully and sensitively following yourself and the others, trying to grasp and understand, to unite in a perfect harmony of music and thought. That's what is so inspiring about music, that it excites and conveys all the wealth of a man's thoughts and at the same time creates a ravishing human solidarity."

"And, by thunder, that was beautifully put!" Schächter said, grinning. "What a pity I can't talk like that: maybe they'd have made me a Court Councilor, too. But he's right about one thing," he admitted: "you wouldn't believe how much of all that I can say with music from behind the conductor's rostrum, how many real memories it calls up, how many griefs it consoles, how much it stiffens courage and resistance. What I'm saying is that music is magic. And sometimes when I'm at rehearsals music stops being magic. Then I know at once that something's wrong, somewhere there's an obstruction, either in the accord with the conductor or as now, when we've progressed so far, in the conductor himself. I confirm, I doubt, I seek, I rediscover. I am now the weakest member of the whole company. Bear that in mind, please, and have patience with me."

The Court Councilor watched Schächter fixedly; he could not hear very well what he was saying, and even if he had heard, he did not understand Czech. In spite of that, however, he at once put in a word.

"You have a new tenor," he explained. "He dropped among you suddenly, as though from heaven, quite unexpectedly. He came to you as from another world, bringing you messages from Verdi's Italy, and he sings as they understand singing there. He must get accustomed to you, and with his singing he has brought you so much that is evocative, a new mine for you to open and use and conquer. Then will come the end of the long preparations, then your conductor can place himself confidently at your head, so that you and he together, in a single assault, may storm and carry away the last force, which remains to the artist unknown and incalculable, to which he must react directly and impulsively, without which he cannot perfect his work.

"And this force, which to the last moment heightens the drama of artistic utterance, and together with you will determine the final form of the work . . . is the public."

"Tomorrow we'll run through some of the tenor parts once more. The second part of the choir and the soloists will come to rehearsal. And that's the last time I shall be rehearsing like this, really the last. Next time we'll pass to rehearsals with the complete ensemble," Schächter assured them all.

The singers didn't believe him: in their full numbers they wouldn't even be able to get into the cellar. But they came to the rehearsal. Punctually. Only Cherubino was missing. They waited for him a quarter of an hour, half an hour. Then they gave up expecting him. They knew.

He had not escaped Haindl, after all. The familiar road awaited him. A summons to Command Headquarters, the torture chamber in the underground cells, the casemates of the Little Fortress, and then Auschwitz, if he endured so long.

They sat there wretchedly, no one saying a word. It was inevitable that it should come to this; they had always dreaded it. Nothing else was possible; one day he would surely vanish as suddenly as he had appeared among them, a messenger from another world, from Italy, the land of the sun and of song. They would never forget him, the boy angel with the street urchin's face, as Raphael and Murillo had painted the angels. And how beautifully that boy sang; the heart melted, hearing him. And now he did not come.

What was Schächter still waiting for? Why didn't he begin as usual, with the fugue of the *Sanctus?* He always began with that when he needed to drown something out, when he had no soloists. They stole glances at him; he wasn't standing at his rostrum but sitting on a bench with his face hidden in his hands. He couldn't begin. This time he couldn't.

The cellar door opened suddenly; the young Jew appeared in the doorway, his face stamped with the terror of the hunted beast, as on the day when he first came there. They looked up at him and no one spoke; mutely they stared at him.

"He's got me," he said in a trembling voice. "I'm going to Command Headquarters."

Why did he tell them that? Didn't they know it? Why had he come here? Why didn't he vanish quietly, unobtrusively, as thousands of them had vanished behind the doors of the sealed wagons? Had he come to show them the body that in so short a time was to be seared beneath the red-hot iron and broken under the blows of heavy clubs? Had he come to fill their ears with the glorious voice soon to be silenced in convulsions of screams and moans? What did he want here? He shouldn't have come! He didn't belong to them; he was an intruder among them, a stray from a far, foreign land, from another world. They had brought him here only a little while ago in *Wehrmacht* uniform; what did he know of the sufferings of Jews in the concentration camps?

"I've got to report in an hour. I still have an hour left," said the young voice at the door unsteadily. "I've got nobody here. And it's been so beautiful here. I've never in my life felt so happy as I have been here with you."

"Let's begin," Schächter thundered, and sat down at the harmonium.

They all went obediently to their places, even the young Jew, as the conductor's hand energetically directed him.

What were they to sing? Who was to be the first to overcome with music this constricting, disabling oppression? To whom would their conductor entrust such a terrible task?

With deep concentration Schächter pondered the question.

"The *Recordare*—bar three hundred and eighty-four," he said gently and calmly, as though they were engaged in an ordinary rehearsal.

Recordare! The choir trembled. A duet for soprano and mezzo. He had laid the burden upon the women. And he gave them no time for preparation; he was already raising his hand.

" '*Recordare Jesu pie,*' " Betka began almost inaudibly, and there the soprano should have relieved her, but Maruška's voice did not come in. Betka sang alone. And now she was ending the verse and embarking upon the next: " '*Querens me–*' " And there the soprano came to meet her.

" 'Weary he sank, searching for me . . .' " Maruška labored with the tremulous words. She could not sing; tears constricted her throat; but already Betka was coming to her aid, supporting her with that glorious voice of hers, a gallant sister of mercy. It was she who had to radiate strength now. Even Schächter could not help her any longer. He had weakened suddenly; he could neither raise his head nor move his hand. But Maruška's bell-clear soprano was gaining strength. The two voices mingled and darkened; they were no longer singing but passionately praying together. O righteous judge, grant us forgiveness, grant it before you cast up the tale of our grievous sins, grant it to Cherubino, who has known but twenty-two years of life, and been no more than a moment with us here in this Jewish camp. He doesn't know yet what men are capable of. Have mercy on him!

Schächter could only listen helplessly. He neither accompanied nor conducted; he could not, for he had collapsed now, the weakest member of the company. And he had promised that there would be a rehearsal, the last rehearsal with the tenor!

And so it would be, so it must be, he agonized without pause. And softly he laid his hand upon the keys of the harmonium and closed their prayer with a deep chord, Now came the tenor's turn. Would he hear him? He could not look at him; he hesitated for a moment with bowed head, and then made an irresolute motion of his hand. And then he heard him.

Faintly, tremulously, but he was singing. The boy was singing!

"'*Ingemisco tamquam reus*,'" lamented Cherubino.

Groaning 'neath my sins I languish,
Lord, have mercy on my anguish.
Me unworthy, Lord, lean o'er me,
Spread Thy grace behind, before me,
Lest the flames of hell devour me.

No Jew could sing like that, Schächter
thought to himself; a Jew never makes confession, he cannot repent thus deeply, or find such
consolation in his despair. Only a Catholic sings
like that, a deeply believing Catholic, and that is
what he is who is praying now and pleading
passionately: " 'Grant me to dwell at Thy right
hand!' "

The verse was repeated, the melody returned,
the singing soared to still more poignant heights
of passion and ecstasy, and Schächter listened
devoutly and accompanied reverently. He would
never hear this voice again. With this tenor this
was the last rehearsal.

"Tremens factus" was the only verse whose
solo part Schächter never rehearsed together

with the orchestra. Always he avoided it, always he leaped over it; only the orchestral accompaniment he practiced and polished meticulously, as though in those repetitive, wavering phrases the whole Requiem culminated. "I'm leaving the solo for the general rehearsal," he sometimes excused himself with some embarrassment; but he convinced nobody. He's hiding something from us, and it has something to do with Maruška, they thought to themselves, but no one tried to uncover the secret. Their minds were fully occupied with something very different.

For the transports had suddenly ceased, and life in the ghetto blazed up into a new hope. Every day Schächter's choir and orchestra grew beneath his hands, for he had always had to make allowances for the departure of people with the transports, and he had built up a great reserve from the ranks of the artists. And now suddenly they all remained with him; not one was torn away. He had to get used to handling a new and giant ensemble; the music now spoke a different language than formerly. Nor did they rehearse in their cellar now, for the Command had freed the great space reserved up to this time for the assembly of people for the transports, and the ghetto had a concert hall at last. There they had transferred their activities.

And then finally came the day for which they had waited so long and so wistfully. General rehearsal! They all came, the performers and the reserves, the soloists, too: the tenor Rosenfeld, thin and pale but already recovered; the bass Charles—fourth in the line of Charleses and, like the Emperor Charles the Fourth, sometimes called "the father of his country" by his associates. He was Schächter's latest discovery, for Mephistopheles could no longer sing; the smoke of the chimneys had ruined his voice. And here was Betka, too, the mezzo-soprano. Only Maruška had not yet arrived, but the conductor did not wait for her; he called everyone to him.

"I want to tell you about the history of one of us," he began directly, without preamble. "They killed her father and mother. Before her eyes. She fought to defend them with her bare arms until her arms were broken. That happened in Munich, in the year thirty-three. She was then fifteen years old.

"She escaped to Vienna after her elder

brother. In thirty-eight they killed her brother. She didn't fight this time, she only shrieked—until they silenced her.

"She had a sweetheart, and with him she fled to Prague. And there—this happened in forty-one—she didn't even shriek now, she only stared mutely.·

" *'Tremens factus'* is one of the most shattering verses in the whole Requiem. A simple idea, it can be expressed quite simply in words: I tremble like a leaf, I am afraid. A human creature whom they have broken here publicly confesses it. Every public confession is shocking, when someone must strip himself before strangers, stand naked before them, and let them see into the most profound secrets of the soul. It is dreadful when someone confesses to crimes, but far worse when he confesses his weakness. I tremble like a leaf, I am afraid! Thus a broken human spirit surrenders itself to mercy or damnation.

"I have heard Maruška sing those words. Four times she must repeat them in the conclusion. The last time she only whispers them in a deep recitative. And every time she lives over again the horror of Munich, Vienna, and

Prague. And now we're demanding of her that she should make the confession publicly: I tremble like a leaf, I am afraid! The Latin words won't help her, the choir doesn't accompany her, and in the orchestra there'll only be the cello drawing out the melody a little. She must tread her way of the cross alone.

"Only once have I heard Maruška sing 'Tremens factus.' I could not rehearse this verse with her a second time, nor was there any need. You will hear her now, at the general rehearsal.

"And now friends, we'll wait for Maruška, she'll be here soon," said Schächter uneasily, and looked at his watch. And after a moment he continued hesitantly:

"I have still two pieces of news for you, and the first won't bring you any comfort.

"This morning our Court Councilor died. I went to the old rehearsal room for the music and found him dead in the cellar. His face was calm and smiling. The score was lying beside him on the floor. They're just taking him away to the crematorium. Maruška has gone to say good-by to him."

They stood silent around him, their heads bowed. But Schächter waved his hands, as though he wished to frighten away the cloudy sadness from their faces, and in a changed voice he proclaimed solemnly:

"And the second piece of news: Saturday will be the *première* of Verdi's Requiem!"

With long-drawn melodic phrases, pianissimo, Verdi's Requiem begins. As when an organist sits down at the organ and with a delicate hand first touches the keys. The cello quietly takes up the melody, and Schächter subdues it still further—softly, please, more softly and humbly. A strange motif, he hears it now as something new and changed; this music speaks with an altered voice today. "Does the gentleman want his soup?" begged the cello very softly.

Schächter was trembling. The music was magic, yes, from the very first notes. No, the gentleman did not want his soup. Moreover, he would not listen to the music any longer; he must fuse with it, for here the choir came in. And others are coming in with them, Raphael Schächter, replied the strings in a muted whisper beneath the bow; do you hear the echo of tired, shuffling footsteps? " 'Requiem aeternam dona eis, Domine,' " the choir whispered softly. Yes, grant, O Lord, peace and rest to those who have gone from us, grant them purpose and strength for their onward journey, and never let hope be taken from them.

Schächter experienced this première as if it were all part of a feverish dream. Every note, every cadence of the music recalled something to him, every voice brought something back to life. He could no longer count the singers with whom he had practiced and rehearsed, note by note, syllable by syllable, but now they were all present in a single great choir, he had them all before him, even those who had been taken from him long ago. All together now they fashioned the final great work.

The kettle drums rolled, the Dies Irae, the first reverse in the general harmony. How many reverses had he not suffered and survived before he achieved his Requiem? How many times had he stared despairingly at the empty benches as upon open, gaping wounds. Always they had torn someone away from him, savagely, inhumanly. Perhaps there had never been any work bought at so great a price. How often had he begun again at the beginning, collapsing with weakness . . . But now they were singing and playing. Listen, you inhabitants of the concentration camps, we endured, we never gave way, we never succumbed. And we've lived to see those others, the damned, near their final accounting. The tale of their crimes has been told; the day is coming when they'll stand before the righteous court of the whole of humanity. " *'Confutatis maledictis, flammis acribus addictis,'* " thundered the bass in awful tones, and immediately the music sank into penitent lamentation. In vain the condemned pleaded; his voice ebbed into the frenzy of the storm. It raged through the entire hall, but the conductor hushed and stilled it until nothing was left but a distant murmur in the violins.

Silence fell. Schächter had himself well in hand; he stood motionless, his arms outstretched. Silence! ordered the arrested hand. Even silence is music; it sharpens the awareness. No one in the hall so much as breathed; they waited with intense concentration.

Lacrymosa! The quartet of soloists, the verse whispered by the dying Mozart.

Betka raised her heart-rending lament, and Schächter did not guide her; he almost stopped conducting. No need for me to teach you, Betka, how to pronounce *"lacrymosa"*: life has taught you that, there, where life in the ghetto is hardest and saddest, in the cells among the imbeciles. And now you cry out your anguish here, you, the soul of gallantry. Yes, cry, then, draw in strength, for to everyone in need you have given it freely.

With a long chord the first part of the Requiem ended, but at once Schächter raised his hand; he would not break the charmed thread of the magical music. He passed on directly to the *Offertorium*, and led his soloists subtly into it; the instruments of the orchestra mingled in a broad flood of overwhelming sound, and with a creative hand he animated them into a triumphant unity, worthy of the conception of a great artist.

And did the listeners appreciate this music? Of that he had no doubt; he felt the deep-held breath in the auditorium, the intensity of emotion. Did they even understand the speech of the music, did they grasp what it was trying to say to them? I cannot speak to you in words, I am addressing you in music, but listen to me, you prisoners in a Jewish concentration camp: The end of the war is coming. We who are the seed of Abraham will tread no more the way of the cross. For you, too, suffering is at an end. We'll walk no more in darkness and insecurity: for you, too, the day of life is dawning. Listen to what the choir is singing to you. "*Libera me!*" Do you understand? "Liberty, liberty!"

How would the prisoners reply? Only let there be no instant, deaf applause; such praise was of no value here. In a concentration camp, he was not contending for that; it would be an artistic defeat. With silence the transported listener would show the depth of his emotion, silence preceding a storm of applause.

Had they understood? How would they answer? A decisive question for an artist. The music soared and took fire, and Schächter spurred orchestra and choir into the passionate, martial chorus of the concluding fugue. And again he stilled the storm, hushed even himself into tranquillity. You'll see, Raphael, how the prisoners will answer, you'll see it in a moment now, only a few short bars. Maruška's crystal voice softly stole upon the air: " '*Libera me . . .*' " And yet again, almost inaudibly, like an echo from infinite distance: " '*Li-be-ra me . . .*' "

Silence in the hall. Schächter was trembling. A sudden faintness clouded his vision, but only for a moment; he had himself in hand again at once, and stood on guard, waiting.

The silence lengthened. Was it success? Victory! the conductor's tired smile prophesied to his company. And still silence; the seconds of strained expectation seemed to him endless. He wanted to look around. The performance is over; do something! Why don't you applaud now, why don't you move, why don't you go away? And endlessly . . . silence.

Laboriously, as though from a clouding dream, the audience awoke to consciousness. But even then they did not applaud; dazed and wondering, they looked about them slowly with tear-filled eyes and then, in silence, rose to their feet. The artists rose, also. The conductor turned and faced the audience.

And then the applause came, like a thunderstorm. It rolled and rolled, growing ever more violent, and nothing could quiet it. Schächter stood erect, making no bow: a prisoner in a concentration camp bows to no one. The hall re-echoed, and the artists smiled delightedly. Only Schächter compressed his lips and knit his brows, feverishly pondering.

He had waited for an answer from his listeners, and now he had it, now he knew. They had not understood! And it was precisely the finale, the last, decisive words of the whole work, that they had not understood. A crushing reply for an artist. "Liberty, liberty," are the last words of the Requiem, and yet the prisoners had not exulted, the word had not inflamed them like lightning, had not swept them away. Feebly they awoke to life, as from a fit of dizziness, as from a sick, stupefying faint.

You've spoiled everything, Raphael; just in the vital last bars you've botched everything. You and nobody else, you, the weakest member of the group. You were longing for success, you wanted silence, the longer the better, and now they've given you what you wanted. You ought to have measured it with a stop watch, you artist, you. Nobody ever received so long a silence as his reward before. You went out after a triumph, even here in a concentration camp, and the great idea got away from you.

The hall was still vibrating, but what use was that to him? You should have thundered before, when you were silent. It isn't Verdi's fault; he had a master's grasp of what a prayer for the dead should be: there somewhere in eternity, where the last note of the Requiem falls silent, there even you, as dead men, set free from torment and hardship, there even you shall find liberty. For that reason alone he gave the solo recitative in the finale to the soprano, for that reason we have this diminuendo from piano to pianissimo, withdrawing from reality into eternity. What an opportunity to induce the listeners to deep contemplation, and Verdi made perfect use of it. But you, Raphael, you stirred these poor downtrodden prisoners deeply with the promise of freedom and then, in the finale, in the very last vital bars, you blew away that vision of desire, far, far way, where there's no return. They listened attentively, and they understood the music truly; it was you, you, the creator, who had not thought out the work to the true end.

The room was still rocking, and Schächter was flushed with excitement. He knew now what to do about it. I must do it, he vowed to himself, I must, I'll remake the finale. Oh, St. Verdi in heaven, forgive me my sin; if you had been in a concentration camp, you, too, would have composed your finale differently, and I will do it. I'll cut the concluding recitative of the choir, the preceding "*Libera me*" can remain as a solo, but not quietly, defiantly, like a demand, a challenge, and then immediately we'll burst out fortissimo, the whole choir, and the last bars will be in widely unfolding harmony. And the accompaniment? The whole orchestra, and especially the kettle drums, *"Li-be-ra me!"* Three strokes short, one long. Fighting blows; liberty is not to be won without a fight. A prisoner will understand such a finale, and such a finale I'll make, and we'll try it now, immediately.

He turned to his company and motioned to them not to go away, the rehearsal would continue. Then, happy now at the uproar in the hall, he stepped down from the dais, forcing his way through the embracing arms of his enthusiastic friends. Yes, yes, touch me and let me touch you, embrace me and I'll embrace you, but be sensible now, dear friends, that's the end of the performance, run off home, we have some rehearsing to do.

Just beside the little park, with its charming statues and its intimate pavilion in the center, stood the living quarters of the SS. The mighty ramparts of the fortress town separated it from the rest of the world, a high wall and a gray array of cleared and empty houses from the ghetto itself. Here in their private quarters the worthies of the SS celebrated victories and drowned defeats, and arranged cultural evenings for the young girls of Litoměřice. And here the Camp Commandant received official guests.

And he received them frequently, for they enjoyed coming here; in these surroundings they could breathe in peace for a short time. Here the air-raid warning very seldom sounded and even if there were to be a raid, they wouldn't have to run for shelter. An oasis of calm and safety; so said the Berliner Moese with appreciation as often as he came here.

Only for the guests, of course, the Camp Commandant privately added, for to him these visits brought little calm. And they might well be anything but safe, too; they might be very dangerous indeed, as well as creating more than enough work and anxiety. Even the reception of visitors was a service function with a precisely defined competence. And the higher-ups would never tell you everything beforehand. You know, my dear—military secrets! You had to sniff out for yourself what they wanted, and be prepared for everything, try to please everybody and offend nobody.

The program would be prescribed beforehand: tomorrow at 10:00, arrival and welcome. They were coming from Prague and Berlin—that they had also written, and the number arriving—but who was coming and who would lead them, that you would find out when they came. As though that made no difference at all to the Camp Commandant!

And further: 10:30 to 11:30, celebratory parade of the garrison. What they had to celebrate, of course, God only knew; it was a long time since they'd celebrated anything. And why celebrate here in Terezín? They never forgot to note down lunch, tea, and dinner in the program, but what there would be to eat and drink, where you'd get it, and how you'd pay for it, that would be your worry, Camp Commandant; nobody here wanted to interfere in your affairs. They wanted dinner at nine. They said nothing about departure; that was so that you could get your mind to work once again providing a proper free entertainment.

And now, Camp Commandant, consider! If Günther brings the guests, you'll have to provide girls, wine, and brandy; if it's Moese, then only girls and wine, for Moese can't take brandy. Best would be Eichmann himself. In the society of the upper ranks, they say he can get quite lively; he's full of fun, laughs, and raises hell. But among his inferiors he never says a word; he doesn't even laugh loudly among them. If it's Eichmann, you can write off the girls and the brandy; you only need the wine. But you won't know the answer until the very moment when the visitors step out of the car.

They never forgot the inspection of the ghetto, either, that's always in the program, but everybody's used to that already, and it doesn't make much trouble. Where the Camp Commandant takes the guests and what he shows them is his exclusive concern; no one ever attempts to meddle in it.

The only novelty was: "Appearance of Jewish Artists." That had never happened before. Maybe it was Moese who had concocted that; there was never any knowing what was in his mind, and in Berlin, of course, it was impossible for him to go to any artistic performance now. But where was the need of long consideration? The ways of the upper ranks were inscrutable. All right, you want an artistic performance at half-past seven? You shall have it. And you'd better put the thing on properly, Camp Commandant. In the end that's no problem, it's just child's play. But where to get a suitable hall?

He had the whole day to make his preparations, and that was enough for him. There had been a large and beautiful concert hall in Terezín once; he would take it over again, throw the sick people somewhere into the attics, where nobody would see them. Then to clean out the building, polish the hall, yes, and air it thoroughly, to arrange the stage, with curtain and footlights, to place armchairs in the auditorium: thirty would probably be enough, four in front, the others deployed behind them. That would be in order. No need to tell the Jewish elder why they were refurbishing the building, that was a military secret, it would come out tomorrow. And tomorrow would do for determining with him the nature of the artistic performance, there was time enough for that. Length of performance? It's to begin at half-past seven, dinner is to be at nine, only a few minutes for the journey, announcements, and all that bull, and then they'll want to brush up before dinner . . .

Length of performance: one hour!

The military order to the SS read: "Evacuate the Jewish hospital."

Armed with clubs and pistols they tramped into the ghetto. Through the streets rang the martial cry: *"Bewegung! Bewegung!"* ("Get moving!")

The Camp Commandant himself, present on the spot and in the foremost rank, directed the operation. He had already hurled his entire motor pool into action. Three tractors with twelve trailers, two trucks, sixteen wagons and drays from the farm, and four manure carts. Forty-eight Jewish funeral cars . . . And countless two-wheeled carts and carriages for cripples. Only the heavy truck was kept in reserve; they used it for carrying the boxes with the dead bodies to the crematorium, and it was waiting in readiness.

But all these vehicles were not enough. Carry the sick, ordered the leader.

The ghetto seethed; crowds of terrified people ran through the streets. Everybody had someone in the hospital: father, wife, child, or at least a friend. The sick were lying everywhere: in the halls, in the rooms, in the corridors, even on the stairs. In their hundreds. And now, come on, get moving with them, throw them out into the street, take them somewhere, anywhere.

All hell had broken out in front of the hospital. Cries, moans, wounds, and shots.

You'll kill him, he has to lie quietly! *"Bewegung! Bewegung!"*

Where are you taking them? What are you going to do with them? *"Bewegung! Bewegung!"*

The houses are locked, the streets closed. Only one way is open. To the attics of the Terezín barracks.

And the attics of the Terezín barracks are enormous. A heavy framework of beams holds the roof aloft and divides the brick floor into a vast maze of dark garrets. Only a beam on the ground is the frontier of the attic, so huge that a sick man would never be able to climb or crawl over it.

And here there is nothing. No water, no light, not even breathable air. And here you are forbidden to place anything, straw mattress, coverlet, pillow, anything inflammable. But you won't easily set fire to a human body.

At long intervals the chinks of narrow windows gleam dully. They neither light the garrets nor freshen the air. But you can get out through them, and make at least a single step. Into emptiness.

No doctor will find the sick here. Nor can the patients call for a doctor. Here you will know the dead by the stench. Old man or child. Truly, no one will look for the sick here.

The military operation is completed. In two hours and twenty minutes the hospital is empty. And the Camp Commandant gives the order:

Transform the building into a theater.

It is an order. Or rather—the cold, measured voice of the Jewish elder hesitated for an instant—formally it isn't even an order, only a wish that has been indicated. The Command would not object . . . They would like it if . . . It's not only the staff of the Terezín SS that will be coming to the performance; there'll be distinguished guests, and they would like to hear this unique achievement by Jewish artists.

The Jewish elder was practiced in softening harsher orders than this one of today. He knew it would not be easy; people measure propriety usually by the magnitude of the scene they make before they agree to an improper suggestion, and artists are notoriously obstinate, and have a bent for comedy. The outcome, of course, held no interest; that was quite clear from the outset both to Schächter and to himself. No one would risk human lives for the sake of one performance. All that was in doubt was the present scene, and the Jewish elder was a patient man; he had a sincere and deep understanding of art, and he would not have wished this Czech conductor to capitulate at once and agree lightly to such a proposition, seeing in it, when all was said and done, a success and a distinction. And certainly for a Jewish company it was a great distinction; that the gentlemen of the SS should come to listen to them, that called for no comment, but it was said that some of the higher command from Prague were here with Günther, and even some of the Berlin staff, perhaps even Eichmann himself.

Schächter sat silent. His forehead was wrinkled, his lips compressed; only his eyes had a dangerous glitter. So that was why they had turned out hundreds of sick people, that was the reason for so much suffering, just to have a theater for one performance. Of course, these gentlemen had come all the way from Berlin to listen. What an honor for the ghetto; no price could be too high to pay for it. And now, when the hall was already prepared and the bloody price paid, they came to ask him hypocritically, Will you perform or won't you?

A difficult decision. First he must get command of himself and control his rage. There were human lives at stake this way and that; it was always a matter of life and death when a Jew stood face to face with the SS. But there was also something else at stake now: a different life, an artist's honor. A word often profaned, often misunderstood. He should not even speak it; who knew now in what an artist saw honor? We'd play you *Carmen*, if need be, for a loaf of bread and a bit of margarine, when our children have gone so long without having enough to eat. *Carmen*, yes, to anyone you please, even the SS, if we must. But the Requiem?

The Jewish elder waited patiently. It looked as though things were going to be more difficult than he had expected with this conductor. And he had seemed to be a simple, uncomplicated fellow, almost childishly honest. Perhaps for that very reason? Would he make up his mind directly, boyishly, or play the usual comedy-drama first?

"I remember," said Schächter suddenly, and his voice was quiet, seemed even to hold a gleam of amusement, "in the army we had a general, a fool and a sadist. He hounded us with drills and still more drills, battered us into the mud, and when we couldn't go on any longer, it was up with you, march, and sing loudly. We tried to rebel, like fools, but that did us no good. So we sang. An order is an order. But *how* we sang? Not even the most modern of composers dares to create such disharmony. You can't order people to have a musical ear. Sing? Well, an order is an order. But how? That's just a question of an artist's honor."

"I have no instructions about that," replied the elder gravely. "I have to guarantee only that you will sing. How—that is surely not merely a question of an artist's honor. You are answerable for yourself and the whole company. And for anything the gentlemen of the SS may do, you will be responsible—to your company and their families."

"And when are we to sing?"

"Today, this evening."

"Then we can't even rehearse! Well, as you wish. But on one condition."

"And that is?" asked the elder quietly.

"We will not bow to them. Neither I nor the others."

"Agreed," said the Jewish elder.

And they clasped hands.

"This day will be inscribed in letters of gold in the annals of the SS garrison of Terezín."

That was how the Camp Commandant put it in his reply to Eichmann's speech, and it expressed what he really felt. This was indeed a happy day for him. Even in the morning it had been a great relief to him when he had seen Eichmann stepping out of the car. And then, the later events! They had proceeded to the celebratory parade, and still no one had had the slightest idea what they had to celebrate. An award of decorations! Today, in this ticklish situation, when for a long time there had been no distribution of decorations to the *Wehrmacht*. And, indeed, Eichmann in his speech had made witty reference to that very fact.

"Distinctions are not handed out lightly nowadays," he had remarked ironically, "but this time they are awarded as by right. To the worth of the SS statistics, bear witness. Here there's no need for reflection: the successes in reaching the prescribed military targets are shown in positive figures, and the language they speak is clear and convincing."

So they had distributed today, for "military merit," decorations, medals, and crosses, KVK, KVK II, even KVK I; and finally Eichmann had pinned on the breasts of Günther and the Camp Commandant, these two alone of all the company, the *Kriegsverdienstkreuz* with sword. It was Himmler's order that they should be awarded here, he said, in Terezín, in the important military sector of the SS, so that everyone would realize the significance of the action that was hastening to its culmination on the territory of the Protectorate of Bohemia and Moravia.

Eichmann was a beautiful speaker, and it was a pleasure to listen to him when he came to hang a KVK II with sword on your tunic. The Camp Commandant congratulated himself. He had not received any distinction for two years now. Eichmann was right: they weren't giving away war-service crosses for nothing these days;

they had to be earned laboriously. And it was just at this moment that they had remembered, in such a period of strain, and everyone was delighted about it. Everybody liked it here in Terezín. Just look at Eichmann: amiable, friendly, a changed man; not even among his subordinates was his pleasure dimmed today.

"Every time a company of SS sits down to a meal," he joked when they took their places at the table, "it breaks some regulation or other." And promptly he went on to invite the Camp Commandant to sit at the head of the table with the highest.

So here sat the Commandant at the head of the table between Eichmann and Moese, in sheer delight; and he had already given orders for champagne to be brought, for this glorious day must certainly be celebrated.

"And how are we going to finish the day? What are these Jewish artists of yours going to perform for us?" asked Moese with interest.

"Verdi's Requiem," replied the Camp Commandant, as he had been taught.

"I beg your pardon?" Eichmann blurted out in astonishment. "Jews singing the Requiem in Terezín?"

The company of SS had fallen silent, every

one of them watching Eichmann with strained attention. The man was twitching, trying to keep his gravity, but it was more than he could manage. He could not get over the surprise, that Jews, sharp and cunning Jews, should be singing a Requiem, never dreaming that . . . Fools, fools, if they had had the slightest suspicion of what awaited them now, they would hardly have found it any singing matter. Eichmann could no longer control himself; the laughter he had been restraining by force convulsed his face in a spasmodic grin and tore his throat in a yell of mirth.

His table companions stared stupidly at one another without a notion of what was amusing him; but their chief was laughing, and that was an order. The company of SS men burst into loud and lusty laughter.

But Moese did not laugh. He alone remained grave and silent, for he alone understood and knew what Eichmann found so amusing in the idea of the Requiem. The Jews would be singing it for themselves as though tolling their own death knell; that was what Eichmann found so funny. But Moese did not agree with Eichmann. The Jews surely knew very well for whom the bell was tolling now throughout Europe: even in the camp they received reliable reports of what was happening outside, and they were not fools. Let's wait, rather, until this evening; then we shall know what there is to laugh at here.

Nor was the Camp Commandant amused. Never before had he seen Eichmann laugh aloud, and what the devil was he laughing at now? And at whom? At the Jews or at him? What could there possibly be so ridiculous in this program? Pure art, the Jewish elder had assured him, a unique performance such as you're never likely to hear again, Jews singing the ancient Catholic prayers from the twelfth century. Surely there could be nothing improper in that. And the Jewish elder would never dare to make a fool of the Camp Commandant; besides, he didn't even know why he had asked him to arrange this show, and had no suspicion that he was composing a program for the SS. But trust a sly Jew and he'll jerk your feet from under you when you least expect it.

But Eichmann had already calmed himself, and he clapped the Commandant amiably on the shoulder: a splendid idea, my good friend, excellent, we shall be very glad to hear the Jews sing the Requiem.

"Gentlemen," he said, raising his voice, and

everyone at the table rose. "I give you our host! To the Camp Commandant of Terezín!"

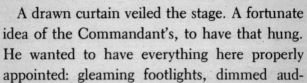

A drawn curtain veiled the stage. A fortunate idea of the Commandant's, to have that hung. He wanted to have everything here properly appointed: gleaming footlights, dimmed auditorium, everything as in a real theater. And he had no suspicion that this arrangement suited everyone; the SS always preferred to stare out from darkness, and the singers at least would not have to look at the faces of their audience.

The stage was full of the sound and commotion of musical instruments being tuned. The singers were already in their places. Schächter wiped his forehead and cheeks with a handkerchief; he did not feel well, and breathing was difficult. This would be a strange performance; they had not even been able to rehearse or make any other preparations. Perhaps it was better this way; he would not even have known what to say to them. Somehow they must surpass themselves tonight— hold together as one and maintain the tempo.

He glanced at Jirka, the tympanist; Jirka would have to help him out tonight. An orchestra has always two conductors; the one with the baton may sometimes flag and lose his concentration, but the tympanist must never weaken. Who could tell what surprises this performance would spring, what the music would conjure up? Perhaps nothing, absolutely nothing, and that would be the best way, simply to play numbly and keep time; such a music today's audience would understand best.

He waved a hand at Jirka: you'll have to help me today, I can't manage a performance like this single-handed, and don't forget, in the last bars there's a change. Choir and orchestra fortissimo, and especially you, see to it! Three strokes short, one long!

He looked at his choir and soloists, and now he felt a little better; he knew every one of them, he knew what they could do, he could rely on them. His only fear was for Maruška; she had the most difficult task today, and to her alone he had spoken in advance. "You must not think of parents and brother and lover," he had told her, "remember the others, too, all those beaten and tormented and massacred, they will unite for you into one great mass, you will not even recognize individuals among them, and so much the more clearly you will be aware of the true face of the murderers. For today you will have the murderers before you. You must not show fear or weakness before them. Today you will be singing to the murderers, don't forget that."

The Jewish elder entered the auditorium and went straight to the conductor. They talked together agitatedly. Tonight's performance must not last more than an hour at the longest, so the Camp Commandant had just ordered. He would have to shorten the Requiem somehow, leave out some part of it.

Schächter stormed and gesticulated. "Scoundrels, villains," he shouted into the hum of the tuning instruments, "they ruin everything they touch, they can't even keep their hands off a work of art." This order hit him like a blow, but perhaps even that was just as well; let them all see what sort of an audience they had today.

Red in the face, he mounted his rostrum. "We're shortening the Requiem, by order of the Camp Commandant."

The orchestra fell silent, waiting confusedly for their conductor's decision.

We'll cut the beginning, thought Schächter,

and begin somewhere in the middle. And already he knew where. "*Confutatis maledictis* . . ." Yes, we'll begin there, damn you, that very verse we'll hurl into your faces. He longed to give the signal on the spot, but he hesitated. No, it wouldn't do; he couldn't begin like that. Better if they warmed up and sang themselves in first. He must not begin like that, he admitted on reflection; he was answerable for tonight's performance to the artists and their families. And Moese was here, and he understood music; there would be a terrible revenge for an insult so transparent. All the same, he wouldn't let them off that verse; he would yet throw it in their faces.

He heard the murmur of movement and voices from the auditorium, the penetrating announcement of the Commandant, and that was sign enough; in another moment the auditorium would be darkened and the curtains would swing apart. How should he begin? Whom should he choose, on whom should he call to stand up and be the first to overcome the paralyzing cold emanating from the dark auditorium?

"The *Recordare*," he whispered.

"Schächter's gone mad," muttered the choir.

"He's chosen the women, he's beginning the same way as *that day!*"

The curtain parted, and uncovered menacing, repellent darkness. The footlights gleamed. The conductor stood erect, facing his choir. No one moved.

On the stage the Jewish elder entered. Thin and pale, he walked slowly to the edge of the stage. And bowed deeply.

"'Weary he sank, seeking me.'"
The crucificial way of humanity.

Tonelessly, in a veiled voice, Maruška forced out the individual words; Betka joined her, and together they fixed their eyes fervently upon the conductor, seeking help and strength. He should have been guiding and directing them, but Schächter's face was white; he stood motionless, hardly living. You're singing accurately, only go on, go on numbly and keep step. So much they'll understand, those down there in the dark. Only go on and keep step.

The duet closed, the orchestra was hushed, and now came the tenor, beginning alone, without accompaniment. Rosenfeld was an experienced operatic singer; often in his career he had salvaged an unsuccessful performance. Calmly he stepped forward from the row of soloists, for this was his solo; his grand aria was beginning.

" 'Groaning 'neath my sins I languish, Lord, have mercy on my anguish . . .' " the tenor's full voice sang, and Schächter listened attentively. You're not groaning, boy, he thought to himself, you're giving a brilliant performance of an operatic aria. That isn't how we rehearsed it. The orchestra suddenly felt where their conductor was leading them, and the singer amended his course. His voice softened and changed; he was praying passionately now.

> Spread Thy grace behind, before me
> Lest the flames of hell devour me.

That isn't Rosenfeld singing, they marveled, that's someone else pleading and praying in deep penitence; his desperate groaning has penetrated even here out of the dark torture chamber under the earth. Your humble prayer didn't help you, child, Haindl got you, and he killed you—Haindl, who sprawls there now in his armchair, stupidly listening.

Schächter had drawn himself erect. He was conducting again; he was in command. Bass!

"'*Confutatis maledictis*,'" thundered through the hall. Listen, you murderers there in the dark, damn you, you and those others a thousand times damned! Moaning could not move you, but soon now, soon, we shall speak to you in a language you'll understand better.

The singers were with him; they understood. The music exalted them; they drew deep, panting breaths, struggling to subdue their fierce passion, to hush their tormenting hatred. The tempo faltered; the orchestra waited. The storm was approaching. They yearned for it, waiting thirstily, until lightning slashed out of the baton, and the kettle drums thundered terribly.

The storm broke, but it did not sweep them away in its fury, for Schächter subdued it. He could not unleash the rage of elemental forces; his heart was constricted. There was one verse he had not remembered in time, but he thought of it now and his head reeled. *Lacrymosa!* He had not said one word of warning to Betka; he had forgotten her.

The storm passed, rolling away into the distance; already the last murmur died away in the violins. Silence fell. Even silence is music; it sharpens the awareness. Schächter fixed his eyes upon Betka, and saw no one else. The silence fettered and bound him; he could neither move nor speak. Feel my need, Betka, he implored, look at me, let me cry out to you, at least with a look, that you must not cry now, Betka, before them you must not!

But Betka did not look at him; she began the quartet of soloists alone. She stared into the darkness, straight before her, where danger was lurking. She was accustomed to danger; every day she looked into its face, always she lived and endured with the mad in their dark, closed cells. She felt the same perilous challenge now; something glittered there in the dark, and she had recognized it. Madmen! These were madmen she had before her, decked out in their tawdry finery, with jingling tinsel draped on their breasts, strutting out their fantasy as heroes.

Sharply she launched herself against them, and Schächter exulted: yes, yes, that's how it should be pronounced, and now that hard "cry" again, and the broad "o," spit it in their faces, cast your lightnings at them. I need not teach you how to pronounce that word, you know best how you must sing.

The first part of the Requiem hushed to its

close, but the director stretched out his hand at once, and bore his artists onward with him. The very music drove them forward now. Listen, you there in the dark, how solemnly the music cries, listen well to what the ancient book of humanity has been proclaiming for thousands of years.

I will multiply thy seed as the sands of the earth. I will bless him who blesseth thee, and curse him who curseth thee.

Do you hear, you there in the dark? You have marked us as the seed of Abraham, and now we, prisoners in a Jewish camp, exult before you. You have not broken us, you will not break us!

Joyfully they sang the glorious ode, but the conductor's gesture again calmed and silenced them.

The orchestra stilled, the choir was hushed. They drew a deep breath and watched with passionate concentration every move of the conductor's hand. The finale began.

" *'Libera me, Domine, de morte aeterna,'* " sand the choir. As though indeed they prayed for the dead, Schächter thought to himself, and was not aware that he himself had willed it so. Dread had him in its grip now, and was draining the strength from him; he could not even lift his glance to gaze before him. Somewhere there Maruška stood; he was summoning her now to the inescapable moment when she would take her stand alone, fragile and slender, face to face with the inhuman murderers, as once, twice, three times before, in Munich, Vienna, and Prague.

The singing of the choir stilled into an awe-stricken whisper, and then even that died in a sudden, despairing cry. Schächter held his breath.

" 'Tremens factus sum,' " Maruška measured out coldly word after word, slowly pacing out her crucificial journey of terrible memories, and again transcending them. There was no one to help her, and she did not tremble. Slim and white she stood, erect, like a statue carved in marble; only her eyes burned, great, dilated eyes, seeing and sorrowing. Again she returned to the theme, again repeated it in a deep, chilling recitative. This was no longer song; this was an impartial judge pronouncing a stern and just judgment. And now the cello softly joined her, took up the melody and sang it in a grieved tremolo, quivering and afraid, Meisl's cello, which had earned bread for his four children and now lamented and wailed its desolation.

But enough of lamentation, the conductor's hand ordered, and he raised it high. Without the baton now, clenched into a fist. And struck.

The drum rolled, the kettle drums rattled, the brass blared, the singers yelled from full throats, the soloists giving voice with them; they could not be silent now. Schächter's fist held back the choir but could not hold back himself; he shouted aloud with the tumult. The last *Dies Irae!* The day of wrath is come, the day for which we have waited so long, and not in vain. Your armies are torn to pieces as you have torn and trampled us, streams of blood gush from your deep wounds, and your country is rent and tattered in the thunder and smoke of thousands of bursting bombs. And this is right and due, not for revenge, not for hatred, only for the sake of human justice.

The storm passed; passion and hatred were stilled. We are remembering you now, our dear ones, an eternal memorial to you who have died for us. And you, prisoners in the concentration camps, be strong and courageous in invincible faith and hope. They sang fervently now, their voices mingling in rich harmony and fusing into a mighty, sublime chorus that ceased abruptly. Deep silence. Their nerves were quivering with expectation.

Like the stroke of a bell, Maruška's crystal voice rang out: " *'Libera me!'* " Everywhere the bells pealed in answer. " *'Libera me!'* " resounded the voices of the choir. " 'Deliver us! Deliver us!' " clamored altos and tenors, sopranos and basses, from all sides. " 'We want liberty!' " the orchestra replied to them. And the kettle drums rolled and thundered: " *'Libera nos! Libera nos!'* "

Schächter started in consternation. No, not yet, Jirka, you're changing the rhythm, that's not here, what are you doing? But Jirka took no notice; he was directing the orchestra now.

" *'Li-be-ra nos! Li-be-ra nos!'* " he beat from the kettle drums. Understand, Raphael, three strokes short, one long; no one who has once heard it will ever forget it. Beethoven's strokes of fate!

Schächter drew himself to his full height.

" *'Libera me!'* " slashed Maruška's passionate cry.

" *'Libera nos!'* " thundered the gigantic choir for the last time.

The last roll of the tympani had ebbed away. The footlights outlined the conductor's figure sharply as he stood erect, his back turned upon his audience. Nothing stirred. Only the curtain slowly closed.

Eichmann sat crouched deep in his armchair, and strange thoughts tossed and eddied in his brain, as strange as the music that had called them up. "Interesting, very interesting!" he observed to Moese.

"Unique. I've never before heard such a performance of the Requiem," Moese agreed.

Eichmann applauded. Not too lavishly, since the artists were Jews, not too faintly, for the performance had certainly been unique, and praise was due to the Camp Commandant, too, for the exemplary arrangements.

Eichmann was applauding, and that was a signal for the SS. Applause rang through the hall. Out before the curtain stepped the Jewish elder, thin and pale. And bowed deeply.

The summer drew to its close, and the time of the transports began again. The Command had promised that Schächter's company would not be separated. The promise was kept. All together they ascended into the first wagons of the first transport.

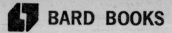# BARD BOOKS

the classics, poetry, drama and distinguished modern fiction

FICTION

ACT OF DARKNESS John Peale Bishop	10827	1.25
ALL HALLOW'S EVE Charles Williams	11213	1.45
ANAIS NIN READER Ed., Philip K. Jason	36624	2.50
AUTO-DA-FE Elias Canetti	11197	1.45
THE AWAKENING Kate Chopin	29258	1.50
THE BENEFACTOR Susan Sontag	11221	1.45
BETRAYED BY RITA HAYWORTH Manuel Puig	36020	2.25
BILLIARDS AT HALF-PAST NINE Heinrich Böll	32730	1.95
CALL IT SLEEP Henry Roth	37549	2.25
THE CASE HISTORY OF COMRADE V. James Park Sloan	15362	1.65
CATALOGUE George Milburn	33084	1.95
THE CLOWN Heinrich Böll	37523	2.25
A COOL MILLION and THE DREAM LIFE OF BALSO SNELL Nathanael West	15115	1.65
DANGLING MAN Saul Bellow	24463	1.65
THE EYE OF THE HEART Barbara Howes, Ed.	20883	2.25
THE FAMILY OF PASCUAL DUARTE Camilo José Cela	11247	1.45
GABRIELA, CLOVE AND CINNAMON Jorge Amado	18275	1.95
THE GALLERY John Horne Burns	33357	2.25
A GENEROUS MAN Reynolds Price	15123	1.65
GOING NOWHERE Alvin Greenberg	15081	1.65
THE GREEN HOUSE Mario Vargas Llosa	15099	1.65
HERMAPHRODEITY Alan Friedman	16865	2.45
HOPSCOTCH Julio Cortázar	36731	2.95
HUNGER Knut Hamsun	26864	1.75
HOUSE OF ALL NATIONS Christina Stead	18895	2.45

SUN CITY Tove Jansson	32318	1.95
THE LANGUAGE OF CATS AND OTHER STORIES Spencer Hoist	14381	1.65
THE LAST DAYS OF LOUISIANA RED Ishmael Reed	35451	2.25
LEAF STORM AND OTHER STORIES Gabriel García Márquez	35816	1.95
LESBIAN BODY Monique Wittig	31062	1.75
LES GUERILLERES Monique Wittig	14373	1.65
A LONG AND HAPPY LIFE Reynolds Price	17053	1.65
LUCIFER WITH A BOOK John Horne Burns	33340	2.25
THE MAGNIFICENT AMBERSONS Booth Tarkington	17236	1.50
THE MAN WHO WAS NOT WITH IT Herbert Gold	19356	1.65
THE MAZE MAKER Michael Ayrton	23648	1.65
MEMENTO MORI Muriel Spark	12237	1.65
MYSTERIES Knut Hamsun	25221	1.95
NABOKOV'S DOZEN Vladimir Nabokov	15354	1.65
NO ONE WRITES TO THE COLONEL AND OTHER STORIES Gabriel García Márquez	32748	1.75
ONE HUNDRED YEARS OF SOLITUDE Gabriel García Márquez	34033	2.25
OUR TOWN Thornton Wilder	26674	1.25
PARTIES Carl Van Vechten	32631	1.95
PATHS OF GLORY Humphrey Cobb	16758	1.65
PNIN Vladimir Nabokov	15800	1.65
REAL PEOPLE Alison Lurie	23747	1.65
THE RECOGNITIONS William Gaddis	18572	2.65
SLAVE Isaac Singer	26377	1.95
A SMUGGLER'S BIBLE Joseph McElroy	33589	2.50
STUDS LONIGAN TRILOGY James T. Farrell	31955	2.75
SUMMERING Joanne Greenberg	17798	1.65
62: A MODEL KIT Julio Cortázar	17558	1.65
THREE BY HANDKE Peter Handke	32458	2.25
THE VICTIM Saul Bellow	24273	1.75
WHAT HAPPENS NEXT? Gilbert Rogin	17806	1.65

Where better paperbacks are sold, or directly from the publisher. Include 25¢ per copy for postage and handling, allow 4-6 weeks for delivery.

Avon Books, Mail Order Dept.
250 West 55th Street, New York, N.Y. 10019

BD(2) 11-77

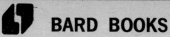 **BARD BOOKS**

DISTINGUISHED DRAMA

ARMS AND THE MAN George Bernard Shaw	01628	.60
CANDIDE Lillian Hellman	12211	1.65
THE CHANGING ROOM, HOME, THE CONTRACTOR: THREE PLAYS David Storey	22772	2.45
DANTON'S DEATH Georg Büchner	10876	1.25
A DREAM PLAY August Strindberg	18655	.75
EDWARD II Christopher Marlowe	18648	.75
EQUUS Peter Shaffer	24828	1.75
THE FANTASTICKS Tom Jones and Harvey Schmidt	22129	1.65
GHOSTS Henrik Ibsen	22152	.95
HEDDA GABLER Henrik Ibsen	24620	.95
THE INSPECTOR GENERAL Nikolai Gogol	28878	.95
THE IMPORTANCE OF BEING EARNEST Oscar Wilde	37473	1.25
THE LOWER DEPTHS Maxim Gorky	18630	.75
MISS JULIE August Strindberg	36855	.95
OUR TOWN Thornton Wilder	26674	1.25
THE PLAYBOY OF THE WESTERN WORLD John Millington Synge	22046	.95
THE CHERRY ORCHARD Anton Chekhov	36848	.95
THE SEA GULL Anton Chekhov	24638	.95
THE THREE SISTERS Anton Chekhov	19844	.75
THREE PLAYS BY THORNTON WILDER Thornton Wilder	27623	2.25
UNCLE VANYA Anton Chekhov	18663	.75
THE WILD DUCK Henrik Ibsen	23093	.95
WOYZECK Georg Büchner	10751	1.25

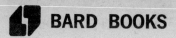 **BARD BOOKS**

distinguished poetry

EVANGELINE
   Henry Wadsworth Longfellow   01669   .60

LEAVES OF GRASS   Walt Whitman   02154   .60

THE RIME OF THE ANCIENT MARINER
   Samuel Taylor Coleridge   36830   1.25

THE RUBAIYAT OF OMAR KHAYYAM
   Edward Fitzgerald   18770   .70

SHAKESPEARE'S SONNETS
   Ed. by Barbara Herrnstein Smith   08904   1.25

A SHROPSHIRE LAD   A. E. Housman   02139   .60

**SONGS OF INNOCENCE AND OF
   EXPERIENCE**   William Blake   18762   .70

SONNETS FROM THE PORTUGUESE
   Elizabeth B. Browning   19836   .75

YEVTUSHENKO'S READER
   Yevgeny Yevtushenko   14811   1.45

THE LONG WAR DEAD
   Bryan Alec Floyd   27615   1.50

Where better paperbacks are sold, or direct from the publisher. Include 25¢ per copy for postage and handling; allow 4-6 weeks for delivery.

Avon Books, Mail Order Dept.
250 West 55th St., New York, N.Y. 10019

BP 11-77

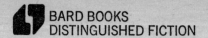

**BARD BOOKS
DISTINGUISHED FICTION**

Finally, in one paperback volume...the finest
writers in all of Latin America are represented
in an anthology which Jorge Luis Borges has
called *"quite impressive. All of the important
writers are there and the stories are all good...
Such a book will certainly be valuable...I know
nothing like it now."*

THE EYE
OF THE HEART
EDITED BY BARBARA HOWES

Outstanding short stories by Llosa, Fuentes,
García Márquez, Donoso, Borges, Asturias,
Amado, Cortázar, Paz, and thirty-three
others

20883/$2.25